How I Escaped
POLITICAL
CORRECTNESS
And You Can Too

Loretta Graziano Breuning PhD
Inner Mammal Institute

contact: Loretta@InnerMammalInstitute.org

Books by
Loretta Graziano Breuning, PhD

Habits of a Happy Brain: Retrain your brain to boost your serotonin, dopamine, oxytocin and endorphin

The Science of Positivity: Stop Negative Thought Patterns By Changing Your Brain Chemistry

I, Mammal: How to Make Peace With the Animal Urge for Social Power

Anxiety: What Turns It On. What Turns It Off.

*Dedicated to
the wonderful readers
who discuss big ideas with me
without defaulting to ideology*

Contents

Annotated Contents

Introduction

What do I mean by Political Correctness?
You spin facts to make the good guys look good and the bad guys look bad. You fear being ridiculed, shunned, and excommunicated if you don't. You often see facts that conflict with politically correct assertions, but you try not to think about them so you don't get yourself into trouble.

Part 1: Feeling the Choice

1. My Moment of Insight (1994)
I suddenly noticed my political correctness when I caught myself lying to my students about a simple matter of fact for fear of sounding right-wing. I always told myself it served the greater good, but now I saw that it served me. It protected me from politically correct rebuke. Once I realized that, I had a choice. You have a choice too.

2. Family Politics (1953-71)
Early experience builds the neural pathways that tell us who to trust and how to survive. Young mammals survive by transferring their attachment from parents to a herd. Here are the experiences that taught me how to survive as I looked for my herd. It's the straight story— not filtered through PC expectations.

3. A "Good" Education (1971-5)

This is not a sex, drugs and rock-and-roll story. My teachers were the most reliable people in my life, so I embraced their world view. It didn't quite ring true to me, but like every young mammal, I sought respect and observed how it's gotten.

4. Saving the World (1975-83)

I went to Africa with the United Nations, and discovered that it was a mafia. I was pressured to make the good guys look good and the bad guys look bad regardless of the facts. I knew how to do that thanks to my "good education," but I did not want to be in a mafia. I kept looking for a new herd.

5. Shaping the Next Generation (1983-94)

Political correctness had trained me to defer to my children and my students, but I started to see the harm done by this submission. I was not meeting their needs; I was meeting my own need to avoid conflict.

6. My Secret Shame

I did the right thing according to political correctness even when I knew it was wrong. I protected myself from ridicule, shunning and attack, until finally my mom genes kicked in. In my quest for an alternative, I studied the mammal brain, and learned that political correctness is biological.

Part 2: The Biology of Political Correctness

7. Why it's always high school in your brain
The superhighways of your brain build from the experience of your myelin years— before age eight and during puberty. Adolescence builds the myelinated pathways that stimulate our happy and unhappy chemicals. No one consciously relies on teen wisdom, but the brain relies on the neural pathways it has. Political correctness stimulates happy-chemicals because it fits adolescent pathways so well.

8. The mammalian urge for social support
Mammals seek safety in numbers because the brain rewards it with the oxytocin. Common enemies bind a group of mammals despite internal conflict. Political correctness bonds people by pointing at common enemies. It offers a way to enjoy the feeling of social support without the messy complications of one-to-one bonds. No one consciously thinks of political correctness as following the herd, but the mammal brain makes it feel good without need for conscious thought.

9. The mammalian urge to seek resources
Our ancestors didn't know where their next meal was coming from, so they had to scan constantly for resources. The joy of dopamine is released when you

approach a reward. But the brain habituates quickly to the rewards it has. It saves the dopamine for new and improved. That's why we're always foraging for new rewards. Political correctness promises new rewards, and shames you for seeking rewards in other ways. This leaves you dependent on political correctness for the good feeling of dopamine.

10. The mammalian urge for social dominance

The mammal brain rewards you with the good feeling of serotonin when you gain the one-up position. We don't admit to this natural urge for social importance in ourselves, though we easily see it in others. Serotonin is quickly metabolized, so we seek the one-up position again and again. That's risky, so we appreciate a fast, easy path to social dominance. Political correctness puts you in the one-up position by asserting your moral superiority and generating new ways to condemn others. But you have to submit to the gatekeepers of political correctness before you can command that submission from others.

11. The mammalian urge to avoid pain

The mammal brain releases cortisol when you see a threat or obstacle. Cortisol makes you feel like your survival is threatened, which motivates action to relieve it. Cortisol is triggered by disappointment, so you can feel threatened a lot even if you don't consciously think that. Political correctness stimulates threatened feelings and then promises to relieve them.

12. The mammalian urge to leave a legacy

Natural selection built a brain that rewards you for promoting the survival of your unique individual essence. Happy chemicals flow, and mortality fears are relieved, when you take steps toward building a legacy. That's hard to do, so the illusion of saving the world is very attractive. Political correctness continually activates the good feeling of saving the world.

Part 3: Life without Political Correctness

Once I understood the needs of my mammal brain, I could meet them without political correctness. I managed to escape quietly without angry confrontations. I do not want war with the politically correct because most of my loved ones are among them. I do not want another embattled mindset after working so hard to shed the last one. I simply want to manage my own brain instead of yielding it to the gatekeepers of political correctness. I will not apologize for that, and if there's a price to pay, I find a benefit to offset the cost.

13. Valuing authenticity

The risks of escaping political correctness come easily to mind, so it's important to be equally attuned to the benefits. Authenticity releases the physical distress caused by squelching your true self. Self-squelching is part of being a social animal, but each moment of authenticity is a valuable release of tension.

14. How to be a good person without political correctness

It's hard to feel like a good person when you're surrounded by messages that condemn you as evil. I learned to define "good" for myself instead of submitting to the politically correct definition. Then I systematically cleared my airspace of those accusatory messages. I can't control the world, but I can control access to my eyes and ears.

15. How to make a living without political correctness

The workplace requires strict submission to political correctness. This leaves you in a double bind: stress if you conform and stress if you don't conform. My strategies for surviving the politically correct workplace are to: live frugally; develop two hard skills; and treat everyone with respect.

16. How to enjoy social support without political correctness

People who talk about inclusion are likely to exclude you if you don't embrace the PC agenda. I did not want to keep playing the same game with a different jersey. I wanted to free my life of in-group/out-group politics. So I developed a long list of alternative ways to give my inner mammal the feeling of support without joining a herd.

17. How to feel safe without political correctness

Like any addiction, political correctness lures you with good feelings in the short run while hurting you in the long run. The habit is hard to kick, but I learned to feel safe without political correctness by: focusing on my next step; avoiding social comparison; and putting things into historical context.

18. How to lead without political correctness

Politically correct leaders win popularity contests by giving "power to the people." You are called a Nazi if you enforce rules, so many leaders submit to the squeakiest wheel to protect their status. Here's how I transcended the beer-and-pizza school of management and honored my own judgment instead of substituting the presumed judgment of "the people."

Epilogue

The day I lost my cool

I couldn't control my anger when I found my new husband in the "blame-the-teacher" school of parenting. But my PC family is gradually learning the true meaning of diversity.

Political correctness puts you in the one-up position by asserting your moral superiority and generating new ways to condemn others. But you have to submit to the gatekeepers of political correctness before you can command that submission from others.

I did not want to keep playing the same game with a different jersey. I wanted to free my life of in-group/out-group politics.

Introduction

What do I mean by Political Correctness?

I do not mean the hot-button dramas that fill the headlines. These are just tribal solidarity rituals.

I mean the belief that we are suffering under a "bad system." Political correctness trains you to feel victimized by bad guys running the bad system, and to fight them by following the leaders of political correctness. If you follow, you get to be one of the good guys and share in the rewards that these leaders control. If you don't, you are labelled a bad guy and excommunicated.

Political correctness trains you to focus on suffering– yours and others. It tells you that fighting the system is the way to relieve suffering. This mindset originated with the express intent to replace the capitalist system with a socialist system, but controversial terms were dropped to broadened the appeal, so now it's just "the system."

Political correctness transfers resources from designated bad guys to designated good guys. Good and bad are defined by opinion leaders who you follow in order to be included among the good guys. The gatekeepers of political correctness have the power to reward friends and punish enemies. But you never acknowledge the self-interest behind political correctness. You invoke the greater good whenever political correctness giveth or taketh away.

You can be a good guy if you submit to the demands of political correctness. Good guys are never deemed responsible for what happens to them. Bad guys, by contrast, are 100% responsible. Whenever you suffer, you know bad guys are the cause, so you learn to hate them viscerally.

Political correctness trains you to focus on suffering— yours and others. You learn to blame bad guys for all suffering, so you end up hating them viscerally.

Political correctness trains you to believe that bad guys get things easily so you are unfairly deprived. Thus your only option is to join other victims and fight. If you question the assertions of political correctness, you lose your status as a "good guy." You must conform to the template of blaming "them" and absolving "us" to avoid losing your protected status.

For example, the student is always the good guy, and the teacher is the bad guy, even when you know the student is up to no good and the teacher is working hard to help them. The worker is always the good guy and the manager is the bad guy, even when you know the worker is up to no good and the manager is working hard to keep things going. The United States is always the bad guy and the other country is the good guy, unless it's long ago, and then the UK was the bad guy. The male is always the bad guy. The white person is the bad guy. The heterosexual is the bad guy.

You must conform to the template of blaming "them" and absolving "us" to avoid losing your protected status.

You are expected to point to "data" to back your conclusions. You use words like "evidence-based," "science proves" a lot. But you only accept data from the politically correct.

Sometimes you are labelled a bad guy no matter what you do. Now you must open your pocket and submit to rebuke in order to sustain your inclusion in the good-guy alliance.

If you don't submit, you will be attacked. Ridicule is Step One. We've all heard the ridicule inflicted on the politically incorrect, and no one wants to be the target of such public shaming. It's enough to motivate most people to conform.

If you don't, shunning is the next step. You are cut off from the resources controlled by political correctness. Much more than money is at stake. Social support, status, and– let's be honest– sex, are controlled by the gatekeepers of political correctness.

Social support, status, and--
let's be honest-- sex,
are controlled by the gatekeepers
of political correctness.

If you still fail to submit, you are declared an enemy. Direct attack is likely. The benefits of submitting are so high that most people persuade themselves that it's "the right thing."

Over time, you submit so automatically that you don't realize you're doing it. You build an internal self-monitoring mechanism to avoid the risk of incorrectness. You censor your thoughts as well as your words because an incorrect thought might get blurted out accidentally. Your self-monitoring is so effective that you even hate yourself when you notice a fact that conflicts with PC commandments.

Yet inconvenient facts keep popping up. What do you do? Do you ignore the reality reaching your senses? Or do you risk ostracism?

A safe solution is thoughtfully provided by the gatekeepers of political correctness. They tell you that the greater good is served by spinning facts because this prevents bad guys from reinforcing stereotypes. So you mark yourself as a person of virtue and intelligence when you re-configure information to make the enemies of political correctness look bad and the friends of political correctness look good.

You don't even notice yourself doing it after a while. Everyone around you does it, so it feels normal. The media lead the way, so you always hear a safely pre-spun story before you have time to ponder the facts for yourself. Your brain effortlessly substitutes the politically correct agenda for your authentic perceptions.

The benefits of conforming are huge. You get a share in the rewards; you are absolved from responsibility for whatever happens to you; and you protect yourself from excommunication. The costs are subtle: that nagging feeling that you have overlooked something important and given away your power.

Your brain effortlessly substitutes the politically correct agenda for your authentic perceptions.
The cost is a nagging feeling that you have given away your power.

But your sensory receptors keep finding evidence that the good guys are not all good and the bad guys are not all bad. What do you do with this evidence? If you have studied cognitive dissonance or paradigm shift, you know that the brain resists changing the template learned in youth. It re-configures reality to fit the template instead.

But they.....

"But this is what *they* do!" you may say. Why don't I write about "them"? Let me answer with a story.

When I was young, I was thrilled to discover the field of psychology, especially the study of irrationality. But I was disappointed to find that this research limited itself to the irrationality of racists, sexists, and capitalists. Apparently progressives could not possibly be irrational. Yet I lived in the progressive world and saw plenty of irrationality. I knew I should blame the system, but my difficult childhood taught me not to trust people who deny responsibility for their actions.

Over time, new research methods appeared but old presumptions were always confirmed. For example, fMRI brain scans are widely seen as "proof" that conservatives are irrationally fearful while progressives are rationally open-minded. I know plenty of fearful progressives, however. You may say they have reason to be fear because irrational conservatives surround us. This thought assures your inclusion in the politically correct alliance. But perhaps you can see that different standards are applied to left and right wing thought beneath the veneer of objective science. Conservatives are pre-judged, in the name of fighting prejudice.

"Fundamental attribution error" the error of blaming our own mis-steps on unavoidable circumstances, while blaming our adversaries' missteps on character flaws. Progressives use the theory of fundamental attribution error to condemn conservative bias without a hint of self-reflection. Anyone who dared to connect the dots would become an enemy in the eyes of political correctness. Few dare.

This book connects the dots: humans are irrational; progressives are human; progressives have the same irrationalities as other humans.

My search for a more satisfying explanation of the human mind led me to evolutionary psychology. I was thrilled to I discover research on the neurochemistry we share with animals. I learned that the mammal brain rewards you with happy chemicals when you promote your own survival, and alarms you with threat chemicals when you see an obstacle to meeting survival needs. These chemicals wire your brain to release more good or bad feelings in similar future circumstances. Our life-and-death feelings about social comparison are produced by the operating system we've inherited from earlier mammals– not by the evils of capitalism. Finally, life made sense to me.

Our life-and-death feelings about social comparison are produced by the operating system we've inherited from earlier mammals– not by the evils of capitalism.

But my excitement turned to dismay when this research became taboo. Academics and the media shunned it in favor of research glorifying animals and blaming human foibles on the racist, sexist, capitalist system. New "studies" representing animals as empathetic were spotlighted. Science converged on the belief that altruism is the state of nature and will sprout like daisies once we tear down our evil system. Acknowledging the conflict among animals, well-known to farmers and shepherds for millennia, is career suicide today.

Acknowledging the conflict among animals, well-known to farmers and shepherds for millennia, is career suicide today.

Belief in a better world is comforting. It's nice to believe that nature is good and we can restore that effortless goodness by fighting the man. It's fun to absolve yourself from responsibility and bond with good guys at barricades and cocktail parties. But abdicating responsibility for your own brain does not lead to a better world. It just leads to the same old mammalian behavior patterns. This is not progress. It only feels like progress if it fills your pockets at the expense of others. Perhaps your human cortex smells a rat, even as your mammal brain enjoys it.

It's fun to absolve yourself from responsibility and bond with good guys at barricades and cocktail parties. But this leads to the same old mammalian behavior patterns.

The mammal brain is preoccupied with social comparison. In the state of nature, social dominance spreads your genes. Natural selection built a brain that rewards you with happy chemicals when you find safe opportunities for social dominance. It alarms you with threat chemicals when you fail to dominate.

Political correctness focuses intensely on social comparison. It is not "change" at all. It is the same old primal impulse, made worse because it rationalizes social comparison as a greater good. You get to feel virtuous with your human brain while indulging in the jealousy and resentment of the mammal brain.

This doesn't lead to good feelings in the long run. It leads you to feel like the success of others threatens your survival. Political correctness entices you with the illusion of a promised land where you are always in the one-up position. No greater good is served by this illusion. Social rivalry becomes more dangerous in countries that pretend to eradicate it.

Ultimately, political correctness benefits only the gatekeepers. I would rather define reality for myself.

Such heresy has costs, but the benefits are higher in my opinion.

Scientific experiments are good, so I like to think about the experiment that political correctness is really conducting. Imagine two groups of rats– a control group that forages to meet its needs, and an experimental group that is passively fed while hearing this message: "You're not getting enough food and mating opportunity. It's not your fault. It's their fault." The experimental rats are rewarded with extra food and mating opportunity when they bite the hand that feeds them. This is the experiment we are effectively performing. Which group do you want your kids in?

I was PC and didn't know it

I was politically correct for decades, but never really noticed. I thought I was just a good person. Then one day I caught myself lying about a simple matter of fact to avoid saying something politically incorrect. It happened in mid-sentence while I was lecturing to 150 students.

I froze.

I was too horrified to continue so I dismissed the class.

Why was I so shaken? I'd like to say it was integrity, but I knew it was more. It was fear.

I feared being a person who could lie to sound good, but I feared sounding "right wing" even more. Suddenly I noticed all the self-monitoring I did to ensure my political correctness. Why?

In the past I would have said it served the greater good. Now I saw that it served me by protecting me from attack. And I saw that an ideology which prevails through attack does not serve the greater good.

Once I saw what I was doing, I had a choice. You have a choice too.

Every choice looked bad as I stepped down from the podium that day. I didn't want to subordinate my life to ideological despotism, but I didn't want to be ridiculed and shunned either. How did I get into this mess? I'm a grownup! A tax-payer! A reader of self-help books!

The books had taught me to focus on what I can control, so I decided to control my fear of politically correct gatekeepers. I gave myself permission to see what I see instead of spinning the truth to make the "good guys" look good and the "bad guys" look bad. I resolved to define the greater good for myself instead of submitting to politically correct doctrine.

Of course it felt risky, but I learned to weigh risks authentically instead of defaulting to political correctness automatically. I recognized the price I was paying for political correctness, which motivated me to pay a price for escaping it. You too can expand your options by reconsidering the costs and benefits.

I didn't want to just play the same game with a different jersey. After my long struggle to escape, I didn't want a new herd that would impose new expectations. This is hard because mammals seek safety in numbers and fear isolation. I learned to make peace with my inner mammal instead of relying on political correctness to do it for me.

This risk may seem like too much for some readers, and too little for others. Some may think we should fight political correctness instead of just escaping it. Others may think departing from political correctness is not worth the risk of ruining your life. I chose the middle ground. Fighting is not for me because I wanted a change from that embattled mentality. And my loved ones are still in the politically correct territory so I don't want to war on it.

I will not tell others what to think, but in exchange, I will not be told what to think. I will not spend my life fighting the enemies of my herd and I will not engage with people who want to fight me.

Escaping political correctness does not mean being "right wing." It means being honest with yourself. You can't be honest when you are dependent on political correctness for rewards like money, sex, self-esteem, and social acceptance. This book shows how political correctness meets those basic needs, and how you can meet them in other ways.

Escaping political correctness does not mean being "right wing." It means being honest with yourself.

If you depend on political correctness for essentials, you are easily bullied. You must submit to each new dictate or else. You may rationalize this by invoking the greater good because it's too painful to admit that you are submitting to bullying to get rewards.

It's painful to admit that you're submitting to bullying to get rewards.

This may sound harsh. It's easier to think you are motivated by empathy. But one day you will catch yourself lying about a simple matter of fact, and you will long for a choice. I hope the story of my choice will help you make yours.

When I was in school, you were a "right-winger" if you believed in open borders. Now you are a "right-winger" if you don't believe in open borders. In my college days, you were called a right-winger if you were against independent schools; now you are a right-winger if you are for them. One thing hasn't changed in those five decades, however: being called a "right-winger" can ruin you. Just the thought of being condemned as one of "them" can trigger bodily fear. Your equilibrium is restored when you embrace the politically correct position. Your brain learns to do this reflexively the way you learn to pull your hand off a hot stove. You don't notice the emotion that animates your political views. You think you're being smart because you're doing what smart people do. You think you're being good by doing what good people do. But you are promoting your own survival the way herd animals do.

> You think you're being smart and good, but you are promoting your own survival the way herd animals do.

Our true motives

The human brain motivates us by releasing chemicals that the verbal brain is not aware of. These chemicals are inherited from earlier animals. They motivate behaviors that promote survival in the state of nature. Your brain rewards you with a good feeling when you do something good for your survival, and alarms you with a bad feeling when you do something bad for your survival. The brain defines survival in a quirky way, alas: it cares about the survival of your genes, and it relies on neural pathways built in youth. This is why we do things that our verbal brain has trouble making sense of. We do what it takes to stimulate our happy chemicals, and then our verbal brain finds a way to make it sound good.

You can understand your happy chemicals if you know how they promote survival in the world your brain evolved in. *Oxytocin* rewards you with a good feeling when you find social support because that promotes survival. *Dopamine* rewards you with a good feeling when you find new resources because that promotes survival. *Serotonin* rewards you with a good feeling when you assert yourself because that promotes survival.

It's not nice to care about self-assertion, resources, or safety in numbers, we are told. So you have to find a better way to explain your natural quest for dopamine, serotonin and oxytocin. You make it a quest for "justice" and "the data" with your verbal brain, but your mammal brain seeks happy chemicals as if your life depends on it.

Nice people don't admit they care about self-assertion, resources or safety in numbers. They believe they are motivated by "justice" and "the data."

The brain built by natural selection cares most urgently about the unhappy chemical, *cortisol*. In the state of nature, threats are more urgent than rewards. Social isolation lands you in the jaws of a predator in the state of nature, so we have inherited a brain that sees social isolation as a survival threat. You don't think that with your verbal brain, but your cortisol surges in response to social isolation, so it feels like a crisis.

You may find it hard to believe that smart people are just conforming to feel good. I found that hard to believe too. I had to be confronted with it over and over and over before I got it. Here is the story of how I lived with political correctness for decades without noticing, and finally trained my brain to feel safe without it.

The Mafia impulse

My family is from the cradle of the Mafia in Southern Italy. No one mentioned the Mafia when I was young, so I presumed it was an invention of Hollywood. But when I got older, I realized there was a blank spot where my cultural heritage should be, so I started doing research. I learned that organized crime is very real. It thrives by rewarding friends and punishing enemies. Mafias prey on their own people by promising protection from "the real bad guys." People tolerate a lot of abuse because they are so trained to fear "the real bad guys." Once they've had enough, they discover that a mafia is hard to leave.

Political correctness is a mafia that rewards friends and punishes enemies. People tolerate its abuse because they believe it protects them from "the real bad guys."

> Mafias prey on their own people by promising protection from "the real bad guys." People tolerate a lot of abuse because a mafia is hard to leave.

The mafia code of silence is not just fiction. In mafia neighborhoods, people live in fear of seeing what they see and knowing what they know. This is my cultural heritage. You have probably felt this fear regardless of your cultural heritage because mammals bond by uniting against common enemies. They define you as the enemy if you don't join.

I cannot idealize my cultural heritage because I know how much damage it did. My grandparents' village in Sicily lacked flush toilets until the 1950s. When foreign aid came, the Mafia stole it. The village finally prospered in the 1980s from heroin trafficking. I am grateful to have escaped that cycle of violence, so I want to avoid mafias however I can.

After my moment of insight on the podium, I did not want to live like a Sicilian peasant, afraid to see what I see and know what I know. I wanted out. But mafias are hard to leave. I respect what my parents did to leave, though I didn't get it when I was young.

My parents did not raise me to kowtow to thugs. They did not train me to protect myself by being an apologist for violence. So when others expect me to be an apologist for their misdeeds, I won't join their herd.

Mafias are tempting because our inner mammal loves the solidarity, the resources, and the power. You get tired of the conflict eventually, but the thought of leaving triggers a surge of fear. So you tell yourself that your mafia is not so bad compared to "the real bad guys." You surround yourself with like-minded people so you only see facts that fit. You suffer, but you blame your suffering on "them."

You tell yourself that your mafia is not so bad compared to "the real bad guys." You suffer, but you blame your suffering on "them."

Political correctness works by absolving you from responsibility. It trains you to blame "them" for everything that happens to you. You can always find flaws in others to justify your choices. But you still have a choice.

Here is how I navigated my choices. Part 1 tells how my political correctness got built up and gradually knocked down. Part 2 presents the biology of political correctness. Part 3 describes the practical steps that helped me escape. There are no easy answers, but anyone can find a way to survive and thrive without political correctness.

You may say I haven't escaped political correctness because it is still there. But I have stopped judging myself against its template. I have stopped letting its accusatory chorus sing in my ear. I found an escape that fits my unique brain and life circumstances. You can design an escape that fits yours.

Each brain responds to the world in unique ways because our chemicals are controlled by pathways built from life experience. Whatever triggered your happy chemicals in your youth built neural pathways that turn them on today. Whatever triggered your unhappy chemicals built the superhighways that turn on your cortisol today. Our all overlap because our common operating system yields common experiences. You can decipher your politically correct wiring and find an alternate path to reward.

No one consciously thinks of political correctness as a way to meet primal needs. Our verbal brain crafts sophisticated theories to explain the limbic brain it's attached to. You have more power over your inner mammal when you know where its impulses come from. Discovering the biological roots of political correctness helped me transcend it, and it can help you too.

Part 1
Feeling the Choice

1.
My Moment of Insight (1994)

It happened while I was lecturing on the Japanese origins of Total Quality Management. A student raised his hand and asked: "Didn't they get this from us?"

I knew that was true, but I didn't want to say so. I wanted to praise Japanese culture, not credit the American military and American management experts who indeed brought TQM to Japan in the post-war reconstruction. I feared sounding like a "right winger" if I said yes, so I said "not really." Then searched for a way to make it true.

Suddenly, I saw what I was doing. I was about to distort, misrepresent, effectively lie, in public, to impressionable youth. It was a small detail, but I saw the underlying pattern. I had been filtering my every thought, word and deed, for decades, to conform to the politically correct belief system.

Why was I pretending to be objective and then arranging "facts" to fit the politically correct agenda?

Why was I automatically glorifying other cultures and then looking for "evidence" to back it up?

Why did it feel unsafe to acknowledge anything positive about my own country?

I could have credited my compassion and intelligence, but that didn't ring true. It didn't explain my reflexive applauding of other cultures and debasing of my own. The real reason was obvious, but I hated to admit it: I feared the social sanctions heaped on people who violate politically correct expectations.

This doubled my anxiety. As bad as I felt about my lapse of integrity, I saw that my fear was justified. I really did live in a world that denounced those who deviated from the "progressive" message.

Did I want my to let this fear run my life? Should I invest myself in an agenda that rests on bullying for support? Was I a person who chose popularity over authenticity?

No. No. No.

But I didn't want to be excommunicated either. What could I do?

I pondered the dilemma with the neural pathways I had. We are all born with billions of neurons but very few connections between them. Our connections build from experience, and early experience builds the foundation that shapes later experience. So let's trace the experiences that left me at age 41 with a world view I could no longer believe in.

2.
Family Politics (1953-71)

My early experience fit a simple pattern: my mother was a rager and everyone deferred to her. I was terrified of her explosions, and as soon as I could talk, I focused on saying the right thing.

My father seemed as scared of my mother as I was, so I learned not to expect much from appeals to him.

My strategy was to stay out of the way as much as possible. I read a lot of books in my room. My mother thought this was "selfish," and her rants shook the walls of our tiny house. My ability to read with this going on was a skill that would later serve me well, though I couldn't have appreciated that at the time.

My mother came by her rage honestly. When she was little, she was left to care for her younger siblings. Her tiny shoulders bore the responsibility of shopping, cooking, and making sure that the food didn't run out before the next payday. She was not the oldest, but the oldest was mentally ill, so she cared for two younger sisters while being heckled by an older one. Their mother was off working in a garment factory and their father was a sanitation worker. He came home from work in the early afternoon, though he was not a man who should be left alone with four girls. When my grandmother got home, he focused his rage on her.

We are taught to blame social problems on economics because other causes are too painful to acknowledge. My grandparents had a much higher standard of living than their ancestors in Italy, even in the depression. But they came from a culture that accepted domestic violence as a fact of life.

My grandmother left my grandfather six times, but went back to him five times. With each separation or reunification, she moved the family to a new apartment to avoid the judgment of neighbors. So my mother moved eleven times in her early life, each time moving one subway stop east from Brooklyn to Queens.

My parents married while my father was drafted in the 1950s. They saved everything they earned at that time and had the down payment for a house in the suburbs when I was a toddler. Fortunately for me, it was in a good school district.

Our side of the tracks had a lot of Italians, while the other side was mostly Jewish. The Jewish families often came from circumstances as bad as mine, but inherited a long tradition of valuing scholarship. Schools were tracked by test scores in those days, and I ended up in classes that were mostly Jewish. I only know this because my classrooms were mostly empty on Jewish holidays. I did not especially think of myself as Italian since I grew up hearing my mother say bad things about Italians. She had bad things to say about everyone. I never knew who to trust, but my distrust of her made it easier to trust everyone else.

I did not relate well to other children. Today this would be blamed on genetics and some kind of "ism." But it's easy to see why the natural intensity of playground politics overwhelmed me. I remember my mother telling me "the Jews won't like you." She never felt comfortable anywhere, and she was passing the baton to me. I did not want to join my mother's war against the world, despite the pressure. I knew in my bones that I got more respect at my Jewish school than I got at home. So I stayed in my room and read. The only books I remember are the Doctor Dolittle series about a man who penetrated the thoughts of animals. And that is pretty much what I went on to do.

My mother never felt comfortable anywhere, and she was passing the baton to me.

A bright spot entered my life by accident: my father started getting free trips to exotic places. The trips were incentive bonuses that appliance manufacturers gave to my grandfather's appliance store. My grandfather had immigrated to the US at age sixteen, and worked his way up from a fruit seller to a store that employed his two sons. When the store earned free trips in the 1960s, my father was the only one who wanted to go. So my parents who never did anything were suddenly coming home from Europe and Asia with tall tales and kimonos!

Then I got included in some trips!

At first it was just resorts, but when I was sixteen I was ecstatic to be brought on a trip to Spain. Imagine my disappointment when I got there and found that we were spending much of the time inside inside a resort-style hotel. I felt like a caged animal. I begged my parents constantly to go out, and to my mother's credit, she agreed to one excursion that is forever etched in my mind. We took a taxi to Madrid's famous flea market, where we shopped aerobically for tchotchkes that would adorn our home for decades to come. It was all over in two hours, and as we headed back to the hotel, I raised my fist to the sky and said, "I will get back here, and I will never stay in a resort again."

I was always trying to earn money so I wouldn't have to depend on my parents. Before age sixteen you couldn't get a job without connections, which I didn't have. So when I turned sixteen, I eagerly took the first job I could find— as a counter girl at a dry cleaners. I got fired three weeks later, alas. It seems I had been making a lot of mistakes, and when people came to pick up their special wedding or bar mitzvah outfit, the item was nowhere to be found. Panic ensued as the store was searched from top to bottom. This all seemed to start when I started, and seemed to happen with clothes checked in when I was working. The manager said he hated to let me go because I was a nice kid, but he had to do it. It would be easy to blame him for some presumed injustice, but in truth I had not been paying attention to detail since I saw it as a "dumb job." My carelessness could have bankrupted his business. I resolved to get another job, and to double check my work.

It would be easy to presume some injustice, but I had not been paying attention because I saw this as a "dumb job." My carelessness could have bankrupted his business.

A year later, my income was up 25%, from $1.60 an hour at the dry cleaner to $2 an hour as a graphic artist at the local Pennysaver. I felt rich!

I liked having work to focus on because my present was drab and my future was hard to imagine. I would have loved to go to "sleep-away college" like my classmates, but it was unheard of in my mother's world. Italian kids lived with their parents until marriage. I dreaded having to stay home when everyone else went away. Fortunately, in my junior year, the guidance counselor called in every family to discuss future plans. My father had to work, but my mother came for the sit-down. I was shocked to hear the counselor tell her that I could get into an Ivy

League school and the State of New York would pay for it. My mother said nothing, but now I know she was the first high school graduate in her family. She refused to drop out and join her mother at the factory, becoming a well-paid secretary in Manhattan instead. She eventually consented to the plan, and so did Cornell.

At the same time, the voting age fell from 21 to 18. My Social Studies teacher invited outside speakers to talk to us about the importance of registering to vote. I remember because we rarely had "grown-ups" in class, not to mention men with pony tails. I remember being told that young people usually register Democrat. I was young. I registered Democrat. When I turned 18, I was already at Cornell.

But first, I gifted myself a Grand Tour of Europe. My fellow students often talked about their "teen tours" of Europe. My parents couldn't buy me such a trip but I figured out how to get it myself. I found a summer program that would cost $1,000, which meant 500 hours of work at the Pennysaver. No one wanted to get out of the house for 500 hours more than I did! I set my sights on that program, and I badgered my parents until they approved.

Paris was the promised land, in my young mind. Everything wrong with America is right in Paris, I'd heard. Paris was happiest place on earth according to the French textbooks assigned to me since age twelve. My French had even been useful when my father's first cousin from Sicily appeared in New York. I was the only person in my home who could communicate with him, and it felt like more communication than I'd ever had in that kitchen.

So while other kids were planning proms and graduation parties, I was packing my hot pants and my Petit Dictionairre.

Young people usually register Democrat, I was told in my Social Studies class. I was young. I registered Democrat.

3.
A "Good" Education (1971-5)

Cornell was paradise to me. Just choosing my own food without flack from my mother was a luxury. Doing homework without her crying in the background was a pleasure. My fellow students did not see homework as a pleasure, of course, and I had trouble connecting with them. They seemed to feel oppressed by their lives for reasons I couldn't understand. They sought to escape those feelings in ways that seemed risky to me. I was desperate not to end up back where I came from, so I found anything that increased the risk unappealing.

In the state of nature, mammals survive by transferring their attachment from parents to peers. I wanted to attach to my peers like any other mammal. But I was never especially attached to my parents, so perhaps I had less need to break away by "rebelling." I was more interested in building skills to survive on my own. This left me rather out of step with my classmates.

Rebellion was in the air, and I witnessed a building takeover at the end of my freshman year. It looked like a parade when I saw it in the distance. As it approached, I saw people carrying guitars and sleeping bags. "Join us!" they exhorted. They were on their way to take over the Engineering Administration building and re-name it "Giap-Cabral Hall" after a North Vietnamese general and an Angolan general. I remember a flyer that said: "Come do your part to fight imperialism!"

I wanted to do my part, but I did not want to spend the night in one of those sleeping bags. I looked for another way, and discovered a whole course on imperialism. I took the course, and when it was over I accidentally met one of the takeover leaders at a party. He was the campus equivalent of a rock star. I pranced over with newfound pride in my knowledge of imperialism and neocolonialism. But the rock star was curiously uninterested. I was having trouble finding my place in the world.

Teachers had always been the reliable resource in my life, so I looked toward them. I was an inter-disciplinary social science major, so my teachers had a wide range of specialties. However, I felt like I was hearing the same message in every class: "We are all suffering under a bad system, and we could easily fix it but right-wingers are blocking the way." They would say this with statistics that suggested objectivity, and with sarcasm that revealed strong emotion. I soon found myself speaking in the same way.

My teachers made it clear that liberals are the good guys, and "right-wingers" are ruining things for everyone. I didn't even have to think about which side I was on. I wanted to be good. I desperately needed a way to be accepted as a good person because I had grown up hearing my mother blame her rages on my failure of compassion. Now, my teachers had given me a sure way to qualify as a "compassionate" person.

But much of their cosmology did not ring true to me. For example, "suburbia" was condemned as the source of all evil. Though I joined in the sneering, I knew there were much worse places than suburbia. We were taught that men are the problem and all would be great if women ran the world. This did not fit my life experience at all. We were taught to blame "consumerism" for our frustrations, but I thought this problem could easily be solved by not buying stuff. I knew my family's unhappiness was not caused by consumerism.

I wanted to know the deeper causes of suffering, and nothing I heard struck a chord. So instead of investing myself in someone else's war with the world, I kept searching. I didn't actively object to what I was taught, but I didn't actively commit to it either. I absorbed it the way you would learn a language so you could talk with the natives.

There was only one message that I could not get behind: the assertion that all violence is "our" fault because "we" are part of the bad system that caused it. I did not appreciate being blamed for other people's violence. I did not believe that a greater good is served by absolving violent people from responsibility for their actions. When I was young, my mother blamed me for the fact that she was hitting me. After grappling with that double bind my whole life, I would not let it suck me in again. I knew this made me a "bad person" in the eyes of the world I now lived in, and I hated being labeled that. But the alternative felt worse.

> I did not appreciate being blamed for other people's violence, and I didn't believe a greater good is served by absolving violent people from responsibility for their actions.

A social science education prepares you to marshal evidence in support of an argument. We were taught to support our conclusions with data, but I could see that your data would not really be scrutinized if you said "our society is the problem." You were safe as long as you interpreted evidence in a way that made "the weak" look good and "the strong" look bad. So a person could coast through college by automatically championing the little guy regardless of the facts. Before "critical theory" caught on, it was clear that criticizing authority was what it took to please my teachers.

I did not coast. I did all the work because I was eager to escape what I came from. But I didn't ask for trouble by going off message- except for two essays that I'm still proud of. Otherwise, I honed the skill of critiquing the system, and envisioning the utopia that will prevail when we change the system. I didn't back this up with citations from Karl Marx the way my textbooks did. I didn't say it with self-righteous anger like a liberal arts major. I framed it as a empirical inference, like my professors.

Karl Marx was cited in most of the readings in most of my courses. I learned that our goal is to build an army of discontent to spark a revolution. I learned that religion is the opiate of the masses, soothing the anger that we should be cultivating to spark revolution. I learned that people who quote Marx are labelled "brilliant." I never felt the need to fake intelligence–perhaps because I read my assignments so I wasn't trying to sound like I did. But I did stop going to church. I had never really felt it, since the god I had learned about was on my mother's side. now I was surrounded by a new set of scriptures. Faking two different belief systems was more than I could handle so I chose the one that was reinforced by my new world.

I learned that people who quote Marx are labelled "brilliant." I was surrounded by a new set of scriptures.

Like most young people, I absorbed the idea that "saving the world" is the only respectable career path. I was very susceptible to the rescue meme because I had failed to rescue my mother. Saving the world eased my guilt about giving up on her.

But I still had no vision for my future– just a terror of going home. I fell back on my old habit of working at part time jobs and spending the money on travel. By the end of junior year I had been to Europe four times and it didn't get me high any more. I scanned for new horizons, I that led me to the perfect career: foreign aid. You get paid to travel widely and still get credentials as a "good person." Sign me up!

A PhD seemed necessary to get into the foreign aid biz, so despite my mixed feelings about academia, I signed up for another tour of duty.

4.
Saving the World (1975-83)

I enrolled in an Economic Development program at Tufts University's Fletcher School of Law and Diplomacy. I went to Haiti for an internship my first summer, and to Africa after completing the Master's Degree. Both assignments went badly because I was given no work to do.

In Haiti, I was the liaison between a project evaluation team and the project's sponsor, the US Agency for International Development. Project evaluation is a routine part of foreign aid because it promotes the wise expenditure of public funds. Historically, project evaluators were highly paid consultants because the job requires technical, financial and social skills, long stays away from home, and resistance to improper influence from those being evaluated. But these highly paid consultants were being criticized by recipient governments, who insisted that their own citizens be hired as project evaluators. AID agreed, and my internship-seeking letter landed on the desk of the AID officer responsible for establishing an evaluation team for a Haitian community development project. He offered to make me AID's liaison to the team, on a volunteer basis. I rushed to Port-au-Prince, where he gave me a fat stack of paper about the project and then departed the country for good.

I tried to contact the other project evaluators— Haitians with PhDs in Sociology, but they didn't respond. We were supposed to be gathering data on how many roads, schools, and clinics were built with project funds. Finally they told me we didn't need to meet because the report was not due for ten weeks. I said I had to be back at school in eight weeks, so could we at least meet to assign me a chunk of the work. Weeks went by with no reply. Finally, just before my departure, they held a meeting in which they refused to speak French, the language we all knew, and only spoke the local Creole. They voted to do the work in Weeks 9 and 10. My 22-year-old, five-foot-two contribution was apparently not wanted.

Things went even worse in Africa. I was sent by United Nations Volunteers to be a junior assistant to the UN's Economic Planning Team in Central African Republic. I knew something was wrong the moment I walked into the office. A group of European economists were whispering in a huddle and no one looked up. I stood at the door for a long time, and finally someone came over and said, "Please excuse us. We just heard that our colleagues fled the country in the middle of the night."

It was the United Nations demography team, there to count the population. They found two million, but the nation's dictator (the infamous Bokassa who crowned himself emperor shortly thereafter) commanded them to report three million. That would have raised his foreign aid by 50%. When they refused, he threatened to jail them, so they left under cover of darkness. I don't know where they went, but the only border nearby was the Congo.

My project did not fare much better. We were sent to build the government's accounting system, but the dictator was in the habit of running the country out of his pocket. Asking questions about where the money went would land a person in jail, so my project was at a standstill. It was not politically correct to say that, so a building full of highly-paid international economists went to work each day and did nothing.

This was hard for me to make sense of. I remember questioning my local counterpart about it, not realizing that local staff were even more at risk of being jailed than expatriates. In my politest French, I asked why the project was paused and he said that we didn't have the data. I asked why, and I will never forget his answer because I worked so hard to decode it. He said "*on ne peut pas mettre la main dessus*," which literally means "one can't put one's hand on it." This is the brilliantly ambiguous answer of someone who doesn't want to go to jail but has nowhere to escape to.

In my copious free time, I got on my United Nations moped and visited new acquaintances at their projects. I was shocked to find them stalled too, and likewise afraid to talk about it. I pressed for information and it was always the same story of host country nationals disappearing project resources. Most of my colleagues had prior postings to other countries where they'd had similar experiences.

They'd always excuse this in the same way: "it's our fault because we haven't asked them what they want." To me it was obvious what they wanted: cash with no strings attached. And we were giving it.

We'd be accused of racism and lose our glamorous careers if we acknowledged what was going on. Did I care? Did I want to be a "professional" who lived a fraud day in and day out? I got a transfer to another country and when the same thing happened, I decided this is not the career for me. I couldn't spend my life doing nothing and saying "it's really our fault." I would still be a "good guy" on paper, but I'd know I was helping the bad guys. I could not join that mafia, so I quit my two-year contract after one year and went home.

My parents picked me up at the airport and I was soon back in suburbia. I was determined to escape fast– so fast that I answered "yes" to the question "can you type?" But I told the recruiter I was used to a French typewriter, so I needed two days to adjust before taking the typing test. In those two days, my resume landed on the desk of the planning director of a Japanese trading company in Manhattan. He needed a research assistant, and this happy accident began my education in Japanese business. It was the new hot topic in academia, and the perfect new direction for my PhD.

This was a hard call, however. Entering the business world destroys your credentials as a good person in the mindset I'd been trained in. I'd be joining the enemy, from a politically correct perspective. This view was not just in my mind– it was plainly visible in the cafeteria at my graduate school. The anti-capitalism crowd sat on one side and the business-friendly crowd sat on the other side. Most people stuck to their own kind the way a gazelle with one stripe on its butt segregates itself from gazelles with two stripes on their butts. I flitted among the tables, not because I was more evolved, but because I had never learned to belong.

Most people stuck to their own kind the way a gazelle with one stripe on its butt segregates itself from gazelles with two stripes on their butts.

I told myselfI this participation in capitalism was a chance to "bore from within," as Leon Trotsky advised us. But I was actually starting to see the value of business. When it takes people's money, it has to do the work or lose the business. This was a much higher standard than the non-profit world seemed to hold itself to. I didn't dare say that to anyone for fear of being condemned as a "right winger." I was even afraid to think it. So I resorted to my skill at mincing words.

I'd been taught to debate the "trade versus aid" path to development, so I saw this as a move on that path.

To speed up my PhD, I wrote my Masters Thesis on Japan while working at the Japanese company. This landed me back in the twilight zone between academic ideals and my true perceptions. By day I was a witness to Japanese corporate drama, while at night I read an idealized version of Japanese management in books. My boss often complained about the jerks he worked with, and I didn't dare tell him about the academic glorification of them. Then I went home and wrote about the virtues of Japanese economic policy without mentioning my real-life experience.

I was starting to see the value of business. When it takes your money, it has to do the work or lose the business. This was a higher standard than I found in the non-profit world.

I stopped working for a year to complete PhD requirements at Tufts. When I reached "all but dissertation" status, I looked for a job I could do while writing the dissertation at night. The hot job at the time was international banking. This was the epitome of evil on one side of cafeteria, but an exciting opportunity on the other. I decided to give Wall Street a try.

Finance was a foreign language to me, so I decided to learn it by doing my dissertation in that area. I seized on a big controversy of the day: how to adjust financial statements for changing currency values. The US dollar was fluctuating dramatically against other currencies, and there was no good way to measure the impact. There was criticism of each accounting alternative. Critics suggested that currency-translation rules could help dishonest companies bury earnings (and evade taxes), or exaggerate earnings (and boost their stock price). I didn't understand the mechanics, but I knew that criticism was a good research topic. My "good education" taught me to focus on corporate dishonesty. Today I see how foolish I was to think a company could hide earnings and exaggerate earnings at the same time.

I approached the subject like an investigative journalist searching for fraud. This made an arcane topic exciting enough to spend years of evenings on. I did not find what I was looking for, alas. But I stumbled on something more interesting: cognitive bias. I learned that every measurement rule can misrepresent because people project old experience onto new data.

You may think I am letting the bad guys off the hook. You may think I drank their Kool Aid. But I would have loved to uncover signs of the economic collapse so widely predicted by intellectuals. Instead, I came away impressed by the amount of regulation in the accounting world. And my life was changed when the accounting debate led me to the new field of cognitive psychology. It taught me that complex realities can't be reduced to one number, and anyone who expects one number to tell the whole story is just plain lazy.

I was doing poorly in my Wall Street job at this time, which the reader will not find surprising. I was being trained to lend money to African governments. I prided myself on my research skills, but one day my boss told me in no uncertain terms that I was a sales person. I was hired to sell our bank to African governments who'd be choosing among different lenders. Analyzing their credit risk was the job of someone upstairs and it was none of my business.

I quit.

Do you see a pattern? As much as one might enjoy faulting Wall Street banks (yes, many of these loans did default after I quit), a mature perspective makes it clear that I was a bit of a drifter. I even started seeing that myself. I needed to stick with the next job no matter what. I would tolerate whatever came along. And that's when I started my long career as a Professor of International Management.

5.
Shaping the Next Generation (1983-95)

I started teaching with lots of ideals. I planned to give my students meaningful lessons instead of empty exercises. I wanted to listen to them. I wanted to care.

But I quickly got the feeling that my students were not doing the reading.

They would come to my office and say: "What are you looking for?" I had trouble interpreting this question. Usually it turned out that they hadn't done the reading and were shopping for a strategic alternative. They would casually mention that they were "slightly behind," or "just about to get to it," or "planning to catch up this weekend." But they seemed unconcerned, as if no one seriously expected them to do the reading. It seemed like everyone was just going through the motions.

I started asking questions. Students told me that guidance counselors suggest going to a teacher's office and asking what they're looking for when grades dip. I said I was looking for evidence that the assigned material was understood. I had trouble understanding what could be unclear about that, so I asked more questions.

Students told me that most of their teachers gave them one sheet with everything you need to know for a test. If you memorize that sheet, you can get an A without doing the reading, they assured me. They viewed this as "very helpful" and suggested that I do it too. I did not.

I made the more shocking discovery that most of my students worked full time while taking a full-time course load. They did this because full-time tuition was the same as half-time, so our courses were effectively free once they paid for the first two. Students enrolled in more courses than they had time for with the intention of "winging it"– going into tests unprepared. You can always drop a course if a teacher proves "unsupportive," they said. Thus, a teacher who tried to hold the line on standards would have to flunk most of the class. Few teachers resisted the onslaught.

> A teacher who tried to hold the line on standards would have to flunk most of the class. Few teachers resisted the onslaught.

I discussed the situation with my peers, and usually heard "our society is the problem." I knew what that meant from my "good education." But didn't we have some responsibility here? I found few takers for that view. My colleagues were busy raging at the administration and the government for not funding their pet projects. They saw students as the good guys, the weak, the victims. So everything students do is either good, or not their fault.

My brother had become a college professor too, and he had similar frustrations. But there was a curious twist. At his university, students typically came from high-income families and problems were blamed on that. At my university, students typically came from low-income families and problems were blamed on that. We had all been trained to zoom in on a class warfare angle and ignore other factors.

At first, I really tried to be "supportive." I caved into special requests more than I like to remember. But I came to see how the students who mobbed my office with special pleading were gaming the system. A popular strategy was to ask for a make-up exam so your friends can tell you what's on the test. Some students did this repeatedly, and sometimes even missed the make-up! I often noticed serious skill deficits among these strategizers.

I gave essay tests when I started teaching, but I gave up when a student accused me of racism. Anyone who read his essays would see the problem, but I did not trust the system to back me up. I feared getting in trouble for "judging" his work, even though California taxpayers were paying me to judge. So I switched to multiple choice exams and let a machine do the "judging."

One day a student complained of rampant cheating during my exam. She said it was unfair to students who do the work and it was my job to do something about it. This student was older than me, and took her educational opportunity seriously. I was thrilled to have a reason to uphold standards, so I started taking enforcement measures. Like roaches, the more I looked, the more cheating I found. I invested a lot of time in preventive measures.

At first I felt awkward about my anti-cheating policies because enforcement of rules was viewed as authoritarian in the academic world. I tried to discuss it with my colleagues and they mostly said "I'm not a policeman." It seemed to me that they were living a fraud, but I did not say that. I just focused on running a system with integrity in my own class so I could cash my paycheck without feeling guilty.

I decided to focus a big chunk of my course on a useful hard skill so students would know that more was expected than a boilerplate critique of our society. I had the perfect hard skill to teach them. The value of the US dollar was still swinging against foreign currencies. People didn't understand it so they were prey to emotionalized explanations. For example, when the dollar fell it was suggested that the world righteously condemned our sins and we were going to hell in a handbasket. When the dollar rose against other currencies, it was portrayed as evidence of corporate greed that would send us to hell in a handbasket. I my students about the supply and demand for currencies so they could understand the concrete forces behind these ups and downs.

I attended many faculty seminars to improve my teaching skills, but I had trouble accepting the advice. We were told that students can't listen much so we shouldn't talk much. To me this seemed like an abdication that would bring a massive de-skilling. Attention is our most valuable skill. Conscious control of our attention is what separates us from animals. Education should build that skill, not lower the bar for equality of outcome. Students do not know what they're missing when you lower the bar. They think sharing your feelings and critiquing our society is all they need to learn. My opinions were frowned at so I mostly held them in.

Students don't know what skills they're missing when education asks for nothing more than sharing your feelings and critiquing our society.

I tried discussing this with colleagues and ended up feeling worse. They would tell me that their classes are "full of passion." I would ask whether that passion translated into actual preparation of assignments. They told me all that mattered was teaching students "how to think." I kept hearing the same answer in almost the same words, and it was spoken with pride. I remember one colleague telling me that "giving out degrees promotes social justice, so it doesn't matter how we give them out." My colleagues were marking themselves as good people. I was marking myself as a bad person in the thought framework I lived in.

I constantly felt a double bind: bad if I enforced standards, and bad if I didn't. I might have lived in this limbo forever, but something happened that changed everything. My first child was having trouble reading. I raised this problem in my discussions with colleagues, and made the shocking discovery that many of their children were educationally disengaged as well.

What?

Social scientists tell society how to raise "our" children, and it's not even working for OUR children!

This struck at the very heart of our dogma. We had always blamed educational problems on "access," pointing to Republican budget cuts and homes lacking books. Yet professors' children had plenty of access and still weren't learning. Shouldn't scientific minds look further for an explanation? Can't we at least question the dogma that education must be fun and nothing un-fun can ever be required? Can't we uncover the subtle ways that education rewards bad behavior and thus produces more of it? No one was interested in my heresies.

No one wants to mark themselves a bad person by deviating from the tenet that "our system is the problem." Perhaps it was proletarian chic to have a child on the disadvantaged track. But I saw my child's grief over schoolwork and I wanted to help. My second child was about to start school, which increased my incentive. I wanted my kids to get realistic feedback from their teachers so they could build skills. If I expected that for my children, didn't I owe that to other people's children?

Can't we at least question the dogma that education must be fun and nothing un-fun can ever be required? Can't we uncover the subtle ways that education rewards bad behavior and thus produces more of it?

Eventually my mom genes kicked in. Instead of constantly questioning my own perceptions, I decided to see what I see and know what I know despite the isolation. I could not control the social science establishment or the State of California, but I could stop investing my life in a flawed doctrine. The high stakes for my children were more important than short-run popularity. Parenthood is a strong motivator in a brain built by natural selection. It pushed me to the edge after all those years of submitting to political correctness. I lived at the edge for a few years, and then something pushed me over.

6.
My Secret Shame

Thinking back to that moment of insight on the podium, I realize I was prickled with shame by three recent incidents.

Parenting was the first. I left my child in front of the television a lot when she was a toddler. It was just Sesame Street, I told myself. It was educational. She cried when I shut it and I didn't want to be blamed for disturbing the peace in our home. So I taped each new episode and let her watch as much as she wanted. She wanted a lot. One day I saw how it shaped her mind. I saw her get frustrated when an image disappeared, and then get mesmerized by the image that replaced it. I could see how this trained her mind to avoid frustration by receiving passively instead of focusing actively.

At the time I knew less about the developing brain than I know now, but I should have done more. I was so determined not to yell at my kids the way I was yelled at that I resorted to peace-at-any-price parenting. I was surrounded by messages about the evils of authority, the wisdom of children, and the sanctity of a woman's career, so it seemed right at the time. But as my children went to school, I saw my error.

My second source of shame was my vote on a tenure committee that unanimously approved an unqualified candidate. This person had a long list of political attributes, but no actual accomplishments. We agreed to tenure this person with little discussion. I think we all hoped a higher committee would reverse our decision, but the higher committees were probably glad to have our vote to defer to. No one wants to judge, but we effectively judge those who don't get a job when we opt for political hires. If I want surgeons and pilots to uphold standards in their committees, I should hold myself accountable in the same way. I was ashamed of my cowardly submission to social norms.

I was so determined not to yell at my kids the way I was yelled at that I resorted to peace-at-any-price parenting.

My third shameful experience primed my brain on the specific topic of Japan. One day in 1994, while delivering my usual lecture, it dawned on me that Japan had been in a deep depression for years and I hadn't adjusted my rhetoric one bit. I was still speaking gloriously about Japanese management and cynically about American management. I continued to make snarky remarks about American quality and ignored the boom in US productivity. The US recession of the early 90s had ended but I was so steeped in "critical thinking" that I didn't dare mention it. I feared being condemned as "racist" for noting Japan's plunge, and seeming "nationalistic" if I noted US improvements. The sharp contrast between my evidence-based pretensions and my glaring neglect of facts finally got my attention. I saw that I was spinning information to make it politically correct.

This is where my head was when that student asked whether Japanese quality control methods came from the US. My first thought was to dismiss him as a crazy "right-winger"– a response I'd often heard from colleagues. But a wave of shame suddenly broke over me. Protecting myself from imagined criticism was not a good enough reason to lie, I realized. I had blamed "right-wingers" enough. It was time to take off the politically correct goggles and look at the world without them.

I didn't know how I would navigate the world without my habitual deference to political correctness. I had done it for so long, albeit by default and without conviction. I started reading a lot of psychology. At the time, evolutionary psychology was a hot new field, and it offered amazing insights about the human animal. Most of the information came from universities, where it was spun to fit the politically correct agenda. But I kept gathering details and the big picture emerged: political correctness is biological.

We mammals seek safety in numbers because our brain rewards it with the good feeling of oxytocin.

We strive for social dominance because our brains reward it with serotonin.

We seek new resources because it stimulates dopamine.

We feel threatened because cortisol is triggered when we see obstacles to meeting our needs.

This is why we surge with life-or-death feelings when we see potential obstacles to our resources and social alliances. The more I understood the mammal brain, the less I believed the politically correct world view. Year by year, I grew in my ability to have a full life without submitting to the dictates of political correctness.

We mammals seek safety in numbers because our brain rewards it with oxytocin.
We strive for social dominance because our brains reward it with serotonin.
We surge with life-or-death feelings when we see potential obstacles to our social alliances.

Part 2
The Biology of Political Correctness

7.
Why it's always high school in your brain

Everyone looks at the world through a lens built in high school. No one intends to do this, but neuroplasticity peaks in puberty so our core neural pathways develop at that time.

It's hard to notice the power of your neural pathways because you can't think without them. It's easier to see how they work in others, especially those you don't like. When you think about political adversaries, you can imagine a template built in high school. But when your own high-school template lights up, it just feels true, because the brain's electricity flows down the path of least resistance. It's important to know how those paths got created.

Natural selection built a brain focused on its own survival. This brain rewards you with a good-feeling chemical when you find a way to promote your survival. We seek new resources, the safety of social support, and opportunities to assert over social rivals, because dopamine, oxytocin, and serotonin make it feel good. Humans mask these impulses with words, but a quick look around makes it obvious that people are always seeking resources, social support, and opportunities for self-assertion. "Our society" is blamed for these impulses, but it's easy to see that these chemicals work the same way in all mammals.

Political correctness appeals to the natural urge to promote your survival. You enjoy a bit of dopamine, serotonin, or oxytocin when you engage in political correctness. The following chapters explain why. This chapter explains the plumbing that controls these chemicals.

When you know how your brain works, you can find better ways to feel good. You may say, "I'm not worried about feeling good, I'm worried about the state of the world." But when you know why your brain turns on the bad feelings, you will see the world in new ways.

Our brain chemicals are inherited from earlier animals. The behavior they trigger in animals is eerily familiar. I was surprised when I stumbled on this information since I hadn't heard it before. Research on the neurochemistry of animals accumulated throughout the twentieth century, but the implications were so politically incorrect that it got buried. Researchers in "ethology" found that animals are often nasty and competitive, as farmers and shepherds have known for millennia. This conflicts with the politically correct assertion that nature is egalitarian and competitiveness is a sin of capitalism. So new research was crafted and the old research became taboo.

But the old facts were still lying there waiting for a politically incorrect person to connect the dots. I was that person. I wrote three books about the mammal brain to help people find their power over their brain chemistry. Those books did not address political correctness, however, so there is more to be said. (To reduce overlap, this book has footnotes pointing to relevant information in the other books.)

The chemicals that make us feel good are not designed to flow all the time. They evolved to reward you with a good feeling when you see a way to meet a need. Our brain saves its happy chemicals for survival opportunities instead of releasing them all the time for no reason. This is why life is frustrating.

The chemicals that make us feel good are not designed to flow all the time. They evolved to reward you with a good feeling when you see a way to meet a need.

To make thing worse, happy chemicals are quickly metabolized, so you constantly have to do more to get more. This is why we're so eager for anything that stimulates our happy chemicals. Most stimulators are unreliable or have bad consequences, which is why people are so eager for the reliable boost that comes from political correctness. It gives you the nice feeling of gaining resources, social support, and social dominance, and when the good feeling passes you can stimulate more with more political correctness.

Happy chemicals are quickly metabolized, so you constantly have to do more to get more. This makes life frustrating.

I am not suggesting that we *should* be competitive or follow the herd or constantly seek resources. On the contrary, I'm saying we must understand our inherited reward system in order to restrain it. If we lie to ourselves about our internal impulses, we are prey to externalized explanations of our choices, like "the devil made me do it," "my genes made me do it," or "capitalism made me do it." More pointedly, people who deny their true impulses can believe they are serving the greater good even as they strive to destroy anyone who questions their beliefs.

Our neurochemical operating system has noble origins. Our ancestors had to find food each day to survive. They learned from the consequences of their actions because bad decisions led to hunger. Happy brain chemicals helped them survive because in the state of nature, things that make you feel good are good for survival. In the modern world, we have more information about long-term consequences. Thus we are constantly burdened with the choice between what feels good in the short run and what is good for us in the long run. That choice intensifies the frustration of life.

If we lie to ourselves about our internal impulses, we are prey to externalized explanations like "the devil made me do it," "my genes made me do it," or "capitalism made me do it."

Political correctness helps you ease this frustration. It advocates doing what feels good, and blaming others when things don't work out. This is obviously not good for you, or for the greater good, but it's easy to sell, so it's good for the people who sell it.

Our happy chemicals are controlled by brain structures that all mammals have in common (the amygdala, hippocampus, hypothalamus, pituitary, and other structures collectively known as the *limbic system*). These chemicals turn on for reasons that are hard to make sense of because the limbic system lacks the power of language. It can't tell you in words why it turns on the chemicals. Animals help us understand these responses because they don't mask their motivations with fancy theories. When you know how non-verbal creatures respond to the world, daily life makes sense.

Political correctness advocates doing what feels good, and blaming others when things don't work out. This is obviously not good for you, or for the greater good, but it's easy to sell, so it's good for the people who sell it.

We're flooded with contrived studies suggesting that animals are motivated by altruism and fun. It's true that animals cooperate— they cooperate when it helps them compete, which they are quite skilled at calculating. Political correctness trains you to believe that you don't care about your own needs and only care about the needs of others. You learn to rage at selfish impulses when you see them in your adversaries, but overlook them in yourself and your allies.

Political correctness relieves frustration by blaming unhappiness on "our society." It lures you with the belief that you will be effortlessly happy all the time once the bad system is overthrown. When you know how your brain works, you can manage the inevitable ups and downs without deferring to ideology. The politically correct world will still be there, but you will know that it's an expression of the mammal brain rather than a harbinger of doom.

Humans are not born hard-wired like smaller-brained creatures. We're designed to wire ourselves from lived experience. Whatever triggered your brain chemicals in youth paved neural pathways that turn them on today.

Early experience builds our core pathways because a young brain is full of *myelin,* the fatty substance that coats neurons and makes them efficient. Myelinated neurons convey electricity up to 100 times faster than undeveloped neurons. Whatever you do with your myelinated neurons feels natural and normal, from speaking your native language to getting social support in ways that worked when you were young.

Myelin is abundant before age eight and during puberty. Those first seven years lay the foundation of your neural network, and in puberty you get a chance to rework it. Of course we learn throughout life, but we mostly add leaves to existing branches. The deep branches that control your neurochemicals are built from the repeated emotional experiences of your myelin years.

Our adolescent pathways are obvious yet elusive. They're obvious because they're what you tell yourself all day every day. They're elusive because they don't match your conscious explanations of your impulses. You can penetrate that verbal veneer when you know how adolescence works in animals.

There is no free love in the state of nature. Animals work hard for any reproductive opportunity that comes their way. They persist because their brain rewards them with happy chemicals when they succeed.

There is no free love in the state of nature. Animals work hard for any reproductive opportunity that comes their way.

Animals leave home at puberty to avoid inbreeding. They are not consciously concerned with genetics, of course, but even plants evolved ways to avoid inbreeding. Most mammals must leave their birth group to get mating opportunity (either the males leave or the females leave, depending on the species). They don't think conceptually about conception; they just do things that promote their genes because it stimulates happy chemicals. Natural selection built a brain good at rewiring itself during puberty because that promotes survival.

A young mammal suffers when it leaves home. Without the protection of a herd or pack or troop, its cortisol surges. Cortisol feels so bad that it motivates urgent action to relieve it. Joining a new group relieves cortisol, so pubescent animals strive for new bonds. That's harder than you might expect. Animals typically exclude newcomers to reduce competition for resources. It works without conscious intent because brains that responded to outsiders with cortisol had more surviving children. Mammals evolved brains that make careful decisions about when to accept others.

Survival takes more than just gaining admission into a group because the newcomer is now at the bottom of the hierarchy. A young mammal's reproductive success depends on raising its status. Mammals who stay home with their birth group confront social hierarchies too. Survival rates are low in the state of nature, and many individuals die without passing on their genes. Our brains are inherited from individuals who prevailed. You might dislike the idea that mammals compete for social status, but knowing the facts helps us manage those impulses instead of yielding to them.

The brain we've inherited has a strong sense of urgency about social acceptance and social rivalry. Such feelings in youth pave neural pathways that shape your response to the world today. Conscious memory of those those experiences is not necessary because brain chemicals build pathways without effort or intent.

You may find this hard to believe. Why would a brain focused on survival wire itself in the years when survival skills are so limited? The answer is simple: we mammals are born helpless and must wire up fast to promote survival. Eighteen years is an extremely long time from nature's perspective. A reptile has no childhood at all. They are born hard-wired with survival skills. Reptiles leave home the instant they crack out of their shell, and if they don't leave fast enough, a parent eats them. Few survive long enough to reproduce, but their species survive because a mama reptile can have hundreds of babies.

A mama mammal can only produce a small number of offspring because warm-blooded babies are harder to gestate. Mammals are born with unfinished brains and wire themselves up during an early period of dependency. The bigger a mammal's brain, the longer its childhood, because survival skills take time to wire in.

Being born unwired makes attachment essential for survival. A mouse attaches to its mother for a month, and it's a parent by two months. A monkey's brain is much bigger and its childhood is two years long. A chimpanzee's brain is even bigger and so is its period of dependency. The more neurons you're born with, the longer it takes to hook them up in meaningful ways. Neurons are actually a drain on survival since they use up so much energy. You have to really get your money's worth out of them by connecting them in ways that promote survival. Anything relevant to survival triggers your brain chemicals, which paves the pathways that shape your behavior later on.

We humans are more helpless at birth than any other creature. We take far longer to meet our own needs. This early period of vulnerability gives us a chance to wire our brains from individual experience instead of being born with the knowledge of your ancestors. The experience you wire in depends on what triggered your happy and unhappy chemicals in youth.

You may think you invented everything after you left home, and deleted all that worthless early stuff. But our long dependency period did not evolve for eons just so you could ignore it. Your neurochemical operating system is built from your early experience whether you like it or not.

Young children are so full of myelin that they wire in experience uncritically. For example, if you tell a six-year-old that the moon is made of green cheese, they wire it in as a fact. But after age seven, lower myelin motivates a child to rely on its existing stock of circuits instead of automatically building a new one. If you tell an eight-year-old about lunar cheese, the child will compare your assertion to its old circuits and decide whether to accept it as fact.

Myelin spurts again in puberty, which is useful to adolescents who leave home. A little monkey must learn new ways to meet its needs in a new troop, and humans must too. People moved to find mates throughout history, so they had to learn new faces, new languages, new food sources, and new ways to get home in the dark. Myelin made it happen, and this is why we end up wired to see the world through the lens of our teen years.

You may find it hard to believe that your political views are shaped by old neural pathways. You may feel sure that hard facts are your only concern. It helps to know that we have ten times more neurons going from our cortex to our eyes than the reverse, which means we are ten times more equipped to tell our eyes what to look for than we are to take in whatever comes along. You are not consciously telling your eyes and ears what to look for, but your brain is designed to work that way. You could not survive if you tried to process every detail around you. We survive because our brain sifts the sensory overload for inputs relevant its needs. You are sifting and sorting every minute of every day. That's why it's easy to confirm what you have already experienced without knowing you are doing it.

You can see this in people you don't like, but it's useful to see it in people you like.

Imagine a teenager walking into a high school cafeteria. Their brain scans for opportunity to meet needs and feel good. They do it with a lot more neurons than monkeys, so they have more ability to inhibit impulses and analyze alternatives. But their inventory of experience is limited. It will grow, but only from the lived experience of rewards and pain. Your adolescence rewards and pain built the pathways that help you find rewards and avoid pain today. You don't intend to rely on high-school wisdom, but your electricity goes there.

And now we arrive at the delicate subject of popularity. No adult will admit to caring about being "cool," yet we get wired to see social acceptance as a matter of life and death.

The factors that make you cool in high school are curiously relevant to reproductive success in the animal world: a healthy appearance, a willingness to take risks, and a large social alliance. We are not consciously trying to spread our genes, but a baboon is not consciously doing that either. We are all just doing what it takes to feel good with the brain we've inherited. We are taught to blame "our society" for such impulses, and ignore their pervasiveness in other societies. But despite our best intentions, we crave status within a powerful social alliance because our brain rewards it with happy chemicals.

You don't intend to rely on high-school wisdom, but your electricity goes there.

In adulthood, we retain a sense of urgency about finding a place in the world because the neural pathways are still there. Political correctness thrives on the urge to be popular, and the fear of being dismissed as uncool. It promises a safe path to social power, which has powerful appeal to the mammal brain.

You may insist that you don't think this way because you don't think it in words. But you think it with neurochemicals that make small social interactions seem like big rewards or threats. Old pathways motivate us to repeat behaviors that brought social acceptance before, and to avoid behaviors that risked social isolation before. When other people strive for social acceptance, you sneer at them with your adolescent sneer. But when you do it, it feels like you're just trying to survive.

The factors that make you cool in high school are curiously relevant to reproductive success in the animal world. Political correctness thrives on the urge to be popular, and the fear of being dismissed as uncool.

Political correctness helps your inner mammal find what every mammal is looking for: the safety of social support, the security of social dominance, and the joy of new rewards. These good feelings are oxytocin, serotonin, and dopamine, respectively. Even if you scoff at these needs with your verbal brain, your inner mammal keeps trying to meet them because you feel like your survival is threatened if you don't.

When your circuits release a happy chemical, you don't consciously know why. The verbal part of your brain has no insider information about the mammal brain it's attached to. Your two brains are not on speaking terms because the mammal brain cannot process language. When you tell yourself that you only care about the greater good, that comes from your verbal brain. When you say you don't care about your own needs, it helps you gain social acceptance and thus makes you feel good.

But the happy chemicals are quickly metabolized, so you have to do it again to keep feeling it. You think it shouldn't be so hard. It's easy to believe something is wrong with the world. You long for a better world that makes you happy all the time. Political correctness offers you that, and backs it up with a powerful herd. Such an offer is hard to refuse, especially for a young person trying to launch. Once those good feelings flow, the brain builds circuits that last.

It's not easy being mammal!

8.
Our mammalian urge for social support

We don't consciously intend to follow the herd, but the great feeling of *oxytocin* turns on when you do. This chemical produces the sensation of safety and trust. Neurons connect when oxytocin flows, so anything that triggered it in your past turns it on more easily today.

But oxytocin is broken down and excreted in a few minutes, so you have to keep finding ways to stimulate it in order to keep feeling safe. Animals do this by constantly scanning for the smell, sight, and sound of their group mates. For example, when cows moo and monkeys chatter, they are saying, "I'm here, where are you?" And they wait for the reply, "I'm here, where are you?" Political correctness is a way for humans to stimulate that feeling of safety in numbers. It says "I'll be on your side if you'll be on mine."

Oxytocin is not designed to be on all the time. It's designed to reward a mammal for good decisions about when to trust. Touch triggers a lot of oxytocin, but animals know that anyone close enough to touch you is close enough to bite you. So they make careful decision about who they get close to instead of touching anyone for the oxytocin. These decisions are not conscious; they're just a release of oxytocin when you see or smell or hear something that resembles a past oxytocin experience. Trusting the wrong critter can eliminate you from the gene pool in a second. We are descended from individuals who made good decisions about when to release oxytocin.

Our ancestors survived in a world full of predators because oxytocin motivates you to stay near your social network. Isolation triggers cortisol, and motivates you to return to the safety of social support.

Social bonds have costs as well as benefits though. A gazelle cannot seek greener pasture while it's following the herd. It constantly weighs the survival value of following against the survival value of exploring greener pasture (explained in the following chapter). Each step toward the safety of social support comes by sacrificing a step toward greener pasture.

We'd love to enjoy the good feeling of social support every minute of every day, but that would not promote survival. If your oxytocin flowed all the time, you would go home with unsavory strangers. You'd invest your life savings with anyone who asked. You'd feel no more attachment to your child than you would to an Elmo doll. Instead, our brain saves its oxytocin for moments when social trust actually promotes survival.

Such moments are harder to find than we wish, alas. Betrayed trust triggers cortisol, which wires you to withhold trust in the future. You get a bad feeling at the thought of trusting in a situation similar to a past betrayal.

Betrayed trust is an urgent survival threat from your mammal brain's perspective. If you get bitten by a troop mate, your cortisol surges and builds a pathway that blasts a warning signal the next time you get near that individual.

Often, betrayal is just a disappointment of expectations. For example, a baboon expects support from its grooming partners when attacked by a lion. If this expectation is disappointed, cortisol surges and wires in a bad feeling about those alliances. If the baboon survives, it looks for new grooming partners.

When you are disappointed, your cortisol is triggered, whether or not your expectations were realistic. This wires you to withhold trust in the future. You can end up with a lot of cortisol circuits, and a lot of bad feelings about trust. This is why we're so eager for reliable ways to stimulate oxytocin.

Political correctness is an attractive option. You can trigger the nice feeling of being connected to a large support network just by nodding along with your favorite politically correct media. You think your nod is motivated by deep intellect because you don't understand the mammal brain. Each time your oxytocin sags you can get more from more media.

We prefer flesh-and-blood support, of course. Something feels missing without it. Yet our best efforts often fall short, so we turn to political correctness again and again. It lures us with the message that peace and love are automatic in the state of nature but were destroyed by "our system." It promises to restore the good feelings we're deprived of if we fight to change the system.

We're flooded with "evidence" to support this

message. Anthropologists produce studies depicting early humans in a state of ideal harmony. Academic anthropology represents itself as a science, but its express purpose is to demonstrate the superiority of tribal people over "our society." If you question this message, you are dismissed by the "peace and harmony mafia" that controls anthropology. So it's not surprising that all the "evidence" supports the belief that peace and harmony were the norm before "our system" ruined everything.

If you consult non-PC sources, however, you learn that early humans warred constantly against their neighbors. Their groups leaders often demanded absolute submission and were cruel to weaker individuals. I started researching pre-industrial societies after I discovered the truth about animals. I read the journals written by long-ago travelers. You can dismiss all this evidence as racism, as the gatekeepers of political correctness suggest, but the patterns are overwhelmingly consistent.

Early humans warred constantly with their neighbors. Their groups leaders often demanded absolute submission. The gate-keepers of political correctness urge you to dismiss all this evidence.

The patterns of conflict in animal groups are profound. Stronger individuals routinely steal food and mating opportunity from weaker individuals, and it's only the common enemy that bonds them together. For example, baboons form huge troops when predators lurk, but disperse widely when predator threat is minimal. Mammals stick together when they see evidence of threat, and wander off when threat diminishes.

Groups are thus defined by their common enemies. Lions stick together to protect their kill from hyenas, despite severe conflict among lions. Chimpanzees group together to protect themselves from neighboring chimps, despite violent conflict within their troops. Female elephants group to protect their young from lions, completely sacrificing their independence. The only mammals who don't form groups are the ones with no predators, like tigers and orangutans. These loners avoid their own kind because conflict over resources quickly erupts.

Mammals wander off when threat diminishes. Common enemies define their groups. Mammals with no predators avoid their own kind to avoid conflict.

Political correctness alarms you about the common enemy continually. This triggers your cortisol by evoking your past betrayals. The bad feeling keeps motivating you to return to the fold for oxytocin relief.

Sex is a big oxytocin stimulator, but animals are surprisingly picky about their mates. A gazelle with one stripe on its butt does not mate with a two-striped gazelle because the offspring would not be optimized for survival in its niche. Gazelles constantly scan the butts around them and know what they are looking for. Humans check people out too. Politically correct people quickly show you their stripes and expect to see your stripes. If you do not display the familiar markers of political correctness, you will not attract their interest.

I must confess that my first love was a guy on his way to fight fascism in Spanish in the 1970s. I was not even aware of that conflict, but young female mammals have always responded to males who fight the common enemy. I defined the enemy as the fascists blocking socialism because of my good education. When someone is attractive to your verbal brain and your mammal brain at the same time, the chemicals surge.

Animals don't enjoy the warm and fuzzy lives we imagine. We like to think they are giving each other the "got your back" feeling that we long for. We imagine them having the "all for one and one for all" solidarity we are missing out on. This Rousseauian fantasy is a core belief of political correctness. If you question it, you risk being ostracized from your social support network. It's safer to blame capitalism for disappointments with social trust.

Humans have always created idealized images of the social trust we long for, from epic poems on the glories of valiant ancestors, to religious scriptures on self-sacrifice in pursuit of high ideals, to op-ed columns on the superior values of progressives. Popular entertainment reinforces these idealized views of social support, from romance novels to TV shows like "Friends" to science-fiction spectaculars about unifying in the face of galactic rivals. Your reality looks bad when you compare it to such idealized images. The more you feel like something is missing, the more tempting it is to get your oxytocin from politics.

Political correctness promotes hostility toward other social institutions such as family, religion, and unprogressive friends. The more you release these other bonds, the more dependent you are on political correctness. It holds you like a jealous lover.

A political rally satisfies the natural urge for strength in numbers. If you can't attend a rally, watching it on a screen triggers much of that feeling. Athletic events and music concerts do the same, but political events intensify with messages more relevant to survival. The brain's natural quest for oxytocin is a powerful political force.

The things we do for oxytocin are hard to accept with your conscious brain. It helps to know more about how it works in animals. Reptiles release oxytocin. during the ten-second act of mating, but the rest of the time a reptile doesn't trust its fellow reptile. Mammals tolerate proximity to each other by constantly stimulating oxytocin. We get wired to do this from birth because oxytocin is the chemical that triggers labor contractions and lactation. (In reptiles, it triggers egg-laying and egg-tending.) Our babies receive oxytocin during the birth process, but it's soon metabolized, so mammals lick and cuddle their children to stimulate more.

A child's neurons connect when its oxytocin flows so the sights, sounds and smells of that moment will trigger more oxytocin in the future. This is why the smell of your mother's cooking or the sound of your grandfather's music is evocative; and it's why a young mammal gradually transfers its attachment from its mother to its herd.

Young mammals learn to stick with the herd as if their life depends on it. They don't learn this intellectually because they don't have abstract notions about life and death. And they can't learn from direct experience– if you had to feel the jaws of a predator before you feared them, few mammals would survive. Instead, neurochemicals teach young mammals to fear social isolation. When a young mammal wanders off, its cortisol rises due to hunger. Its oxytocin droops. Reuniting with its mother boosts oxytocin and also triggers cortisol because the child mirrors the mother's anxiety. The mother may also reinforce the lesson by biting her child. The brain strives to avoid cortisol (as Chapter 11 explains), so a young mammal learns to fear isolation.

Political correctness trains you to fear the bad guys outside the progressive herd. You are encouraged to break your bonds with non-progressives and replace them with new alliances. But new bonds are rarely as strong as the ones built in your myelin years. You can end up feeling like a mammal without a herd. Cortisol flows and you are eager for anything that relieves it. Political correctness relieves it, at least for a moment. Each time you bond around shared opposition to "the real bad guys," you build that circuit.

It's useful to recognize the price we pay for social support instead of just idealizing it. For example, you might admire the solidarity of elephants when you see images of them walking in a line. But a female elephant has no choice in life. She follows her sisters and her cousins and her aunts, all day every day. She only gets to lead if everyone in line in front of her dies. This system helps elephants extend their collective memory, but most of us are not interested in a life of following our elders. We break away, and then are surprised to feel curiously disconnected. Political correctness offers your inner mammal the solidarity it is looking for without sacrificing your physical independence. But over time, you may notice that you are just following.

For most of human history, you could not choose your herd. You stuck with the herd you were born into.

You stuck with your family, your tribe, and your spouse, no matter what. (Perhaps changing tribes at puberty.) Your oxytocin needs were met without a lot of decision-making. Today's world lets you choose who you spend time with. People are motivated to find a better herd. But as you strive to build trust with new people, but it's harder than you think. Cortisol surges when your expectations are disappointed, which makes it even harder the next time. Political correctness helps with its clear rules about who to trust and who not to trust. Of course it's hard to sustain trust among millions of strangers with their prickly individual quirks. Political correctness keeps it together by constantly reminding you that "they" are out to get "us." You learn to fear a world full of racist, sexist, wing-nuts, which motivates you to trust your politically correct allies even more.

Today, people are motivated to find a better herd. But as you strive to build trust with new people, it's harder than you think.

The more you need the politically correct herd to feel safe, the more you fear losing it. If you wander away, you risk being surrounded by "them."

You may not consciously hate people who disagree with your beliefs, but they trigger your cortisol. Once those cortisol circuits build, it doesn't take much to trigger them. Electricity zips to the on-switch of your threat chemicals when someone fails to agree with your politically correct assertions, and you're sure they're one of the dangerous nuts you've heard about. You don't want to be seen as a nut, so you display vigorous agreement with other people's politically correct assertions.

In the state of nature, real threats are everywhere so you don't waste energy on small disappointments. But in the modern world, your belly is full and your couch is safe, so small cortisol spurts can get your attention. If someone fails to empathize with you, or your kid is not accepted by the soccer team, it can feel like a full crisis. Political correctness heightens that sense of grievance. It tells you that you've been wronged, over and over. You can easily end up feeling that no one is trustworthy except those who share your sense of grievance. So you keep reactivating that nice connection by picking up a politically correct information source and re-triggering the aggrieved feeling. You would lose this comforting connection if you deviated from the politically correct position on any issue. You don't want that, so you follow the pattern of seeing only the good in the good guys, and only the bad in the bad guys.

9.
The mammalian urge to seek resources

In the world of our ancestors, you never knew where your next meal was coming from. You had to seek food constantly to survive. Fortunately, the brain rewards you with the good feeling of dopamine when you do. Dopamine is released when you find a new way to meet a need. Our ancestors were always motivated to find new resources because dopamine made it feel good.

Neurons connect when dopamine flows, which wires you to turn on the good feeling in advance the next time. When a monkey sees a piece of fruit in a tree, dopamine turns on and motivates steps toward the fruit. Each step closer stimulates more. The good feeling peaks when the fruit is within the monkey's grasp. Then the dopamine stops and the monkey has to do more to get more. First it pauses for digestion, and then it looks for new ways to trigger it. The excitement of dopamine motivates a mammal to keep striving to meet its needs.

You may have been told that it's wrong to focus on your own needs. You may think the urge for more is an evil of "our society." You may say you are not interested in seeking resources. But energy is your most precious resource, and dopamine tells you when you are getting a return on your investment of energy.

Imagine you're a lion trying to fill your belly. You would starve to death if you ran after every gazelle you saw– your energy would be deleted when you finally found a viable target. Instead, a lion waits until it sees something good. It knows that because dopamine surges when it sees signs resembling past hunting successes. Dopamine releases the reserve tank of energy that it needs to prevail.

If a lion waited until it was starving to hunt, it would not have enough energy. Dopamine motivates the quest sooner by making it feel good. Dopamine rewards you with a good feeling when you see a reward you think you can get. This motivates you to keep scanning for good ways to invest your energy.

But dopamine is harder to trigger than we expect because the brain quickly habituates to rewards you already have. It saves the dopamine for new and improved. For example, berries would thrill you if you were on the Oregon Trail with nothing but beef jerky to eat; but if you see berries every time you go to the market, they don't thrill you. And even on the Oregon Trail, they stop triggering your dopamine after a few days of eating only berries. Unmet needs are what it takes to trigger dopamine. Habituation motivates us to focus on unmet needs to keep the dopamine flowing.

The big human brain evolved to anticipate future needs. So even if today's needs are met, dopamine rewards you for finding a way to meet tomorrow's needs. Finding a bigger, better fishing hole triggers dopamine because you can anticipate the future needs it will meet. Returning to that fishing hole every day would not keep triggering it, alas.

Political correctness asserts that capitalism causes the urge for new and improved. It says you are greedy if you focus on your own needs. Thus you fear losing social support and oxytocin when you take steps toward stimulating dopamine. You can solve this by seeking resources for politically correct causes. So it's not surprising that so many people are focused on that. So many young people think the way to feel good is to strive for money that you can give away.

I am not saying we *should* constantly seek more resources. I'm saying we can better manage our impulses when we are honest about them. We seek rewards because the brain we've inherited makes it feel good. When we blame our seeking on externals like "our society," we abandon our internal power.

We seek rewards because our brain makes it feel good. When we blame our seeking on externals like "our society," we abandon our internal power.

Your brain seeks dopamine as if your life depends on it because that's how it's designed to work. But you don't always get it. Sometimes your quest fails.

Sometimes it feels like nothing you do gets rewarded. Without dopamine, you feel like something is wrong with the world. You long for a reliable way to get it. Political correctness offers that. It evokes a promised land of unlimited resources. You feel like you're stepping toward the promised land with each politically correct thought and action.

"I don't think this way," you may say. We believe in the loftier motives that our verbal brain comes up. We believe in its righteous indignation when dopamine fails. It helps to observe this feeling in monkeys. One fascinating study depicted simian disappointment in a way that every human can related to. Researchers trained monkeys to expect a spinach leaf in exchange for a specific task. After a few days, they offered a sweeter reward— a sip of juice. The monkeys' dopamine soared because sugar meets caloric needs more than the expected reward. But after four days of this, no dopamine response was detected. That's because there was no new information. Once a brain wires itself to expect a reward, dopamine has done its job. The brain saves its dopamine for new information about rewards.

This study has an amazing twist because the researchers switched back to spinach instead of juice. The monkeys flew into a rage and threw the spinach back at the researchers. They had been content with the spinach a week before, but now they were enraged by the loss of something that didn't make them happy when they had it.

The monkeys were enraged by the loss of a reward that didn't make them happy when they had it.

This is the anger that fuels political correctness. Your brain craves that new-reward feeling. You keep losing it, and you don't know why. It's easy to believe you are being deprived of rewards by a malicious force. Political correctness feeds this belief. It tells you that new rewards will flow if you fight that malicious force. Each time you fight, you anticipate rewards and enjoy some dopamine.

It's easy to stimulate dopamine in a world where hunger is a real risk. Lions often go hungry and they fail in 90% of their chases. But they keep trying, and that keeps stimulating their dopamine. Monkeys often fail in their quest for fruit. Sometimes the branches won't hold their weight. Sometimes a bigger rival grabs the fruit first. Sometimes they make the climb and the fruit is rotten. They do not expect the world to be other than what it is. They just keep taking steps and their dopamine keeps flowing.

Dopamine is the "I can get it!" feeling. When you get excited about a new job opportunity, or a new romantic prospect, or even a new flavor of ice cream, dopamine creates the feeling of anticipation. But you don't always get the new job, the romance doesn't always blossom, and you can't eat ice cream all day. So if you expect to enjoy dopamine constantly, you are left feeling like something is wrong.

The dopamine pathways you built in youth shape your expectations. For example, when my great-grandmother was young, she had to carry water from the village fountain every day. That would have felt like a reward to her because her mother had to walk much further to a stream. If my great-grandmother got a free cup of water without having to carry it at all, that would feel extra rewarding. Of course, I grew up with unlimited running water and it never made me happy. On the contrary, I'm encourage to rage at the water system by the voices of political correctness.

Early experience shaped my expectations about rewards. My part-time job felt very rewarding because I didn't have to give my earnings to the family the way my mother did. A slightly better part-time job felt even even more rewarding. Going to Europe made me ecstatic, until my brain habituated, and then it sought something bigger.

My children's generation wired in their own expectations about rewards. Many grew up having pizza served to them on the couch. It taught their brain to expect huge rewards (calorically speaking) with no investment of effort. Some of them were even able to entertain romantic prospects in their parents' homes, teaching them to expect adult rewards without the adult steps of pleasing a boss and paying rent. They learned to expect others to meet their needs instead of learning that rewards are contingent on effective action.

Parents and teachers want children to be happy, but children find this curiously hard to deliver. It takes unmet needs to trigger dopamine.

What happens when a young person leaves home and discovers a world that does not serve you pizza on the couch? They must strive to meet their needs with the circuits they have. Fortunately, this is the job their brains evolved for.

A young person leaves home and discovers a world that does not serve you pizza on the couch.

Child labor was the norm until the past century. Children learned to meet their needs by helping their parents. They learned to expect hard work, and most important, they learned the real danger of tasks undone. You freeze to death in winter if you don't stock enough wood in the summer, so stocking wood feels rewarding. If children had to learn by freezing to death, we would not be here today. We are alive because children learned survival skills instead of having all their needs met for them.

The mammal brain is designed to learn from rewards. A monkey gets to eat nuts if it cracks them open. If it doesn't, it gets nothing. Nuts are very hard for monkeys to crack, and sometimes they struggle for years without success. But no one gives them a nut, not even their mother. If they keep trying, success brings the nutrition that reproductive success depends on. We are descended from monkeys who kept trying.

It's important to know what motivates the monkey since it's not conscious concern for nutrition or genetics. It starts when a little monkey observes its mother's focus on a nut. It's mirror neurons are triggered, so it tastes the crumbs left over in the shells of its mother's successes. Dopamine surges when it does that because nuts have more protein and fat than the other foods the monkey has tasted. These nutrients are scarce in the state of nature, and they contribute significantly to reproductive success. Natural selection built a brain that rewards you with a big dopamine spurt when something makes a big contribution to the survival of your genes. Dopamine motivates a monkey to take steps that trigger more of it. It at first it doesn't succeed, mirror neurons guide it to imitate the actions of those around it. We have inherited a brain designed to learn from rewards.

Today, the natural contingency of rewards on effective action is condemned by the politically correct. Expecting young people work is taboo, and even schoolwork is considered wrong unless it's "fun." If a child refuses to do schoolwork, they are supposed to get the reward anyway because it's deemed the teacher's fault for failing to make it fun.

We freed our children from labor to give them time to build more valuable skills. But if children waste that time instead of building skills, there is no consequence. Thus we train their brains to expect rewards regardless of their actions. If we keep rewarding them when their actions are actively harmful, this is what they learn.

I was thrilled when my children wanted part-time jobs in high school because I knew they were not filling their time with studying. But the other mothers in my world had a bad reaction to the service jobs my kids were doing. Fortunately, I had learned to ignore the mothers' mafia. I even refused their strategy of holding my kids back from kindergarten to let them start out "ahead." I wanted my kids to start out learning that rewards require effort.

Every species alive today has found a way to wire its young with survival skills before the parents are gone. Today, adults with good intentions want to give children pre-shelled nuts to protect them from the frustration of trying and failing. Those children get wired to expect the world to provision. They feel like their survival is threatened without such provision. Of course being given nuts doesn't make you feel good. Dopamine is not triggered when rewards are just handed to you— unless it's a bigger and better reward.

When your dopamine droops, it feels like something is wrong. You can trigger it naturally by taking steps toward realistic goals. But political correctness   discourages such individual pursuits. It reinforces the belief that you should feel good all the time for no reason, and if you don't, it's a failure of "our system." You learn to expect the system to fix it for you instead of building realistic expectations. This belief is so widely shared that it's hardly questioned.

Of course you eventually habituate to the promises of political correctness. The promised land doesn't seem to get closer, so utopian thoughts feel less rewarding. The gatekeepers of political correctness try to rekindle your dopamine with ever bigger expectations of rewards.

You can stimulate your dopamine without them when you know how it works. You can trigger the good feeling of approaching rewards if you build realistic expectations. For most of human history, rewards were simple. You looked for food to relieve hunger. You looked for a mate, and ended up with babies who needed more food. Unmet needs were urgent, and dopamine flowed without hiring motivational experts. Birth control has changed this. You can mate without becoming responsible for children. You can attract a mate without proving you have responsible skills. Dopamine is complicated when immediate needs are met. We need something bigger to stimulate it.

Big dreams are now the standard way of motivating kids because they are used to getting their needs met without effort. In the past, a big dream was to be a fireman or ballerina, but more grandiose expectations are encouraged today. This may stimulate dopamine in the short run, but it may not prepare you for mental health and independence in the long run. What it prepares you for is the army of discontent. And that is the core goal of political correctness, as eloquently explained by Saul Alinsky.

A more realistic survival skill is the ability to focus. More focus brings more rewards, from ancient times to today. But instead of teaching children to focus, we are teaching that it's not your fault if you can't focus. Children learn to blame their lack of focus on something outside them: a bad teacher, bad genes, a bad prescription, a bad system. We train them to expect the system to fix it for them. We don't train them to discover the internal connection between focus and rewards. Teachers and parents who make rewards contingent on performance are sneered at, so there are few ways to learn.

You learn to expect the system to fix it for you instead of building realistic expectations.

Once a person's myelin years are over, these core circuits are harder to build. You can do it, but it takes a lot of repetition. The slow pace is frustrating, so if you have a choice, it's tempting to just blame the system.

Teachers can make themselves popular by blaming the system instead of making rewards contingent on skill-building. Everyone can get an "A" in critiquing the system with little effort. That skill doesn't pay the bills in the adult world, alas. So when you are finally stuck with the consequences of the "free nuts" school of motivation, you see it as evidence of social injustice. You can insist that your bills get paid for you by people who have more nuts. You can hate them for having more, and the more they do, the more you can hate them. They may keep paying your bills anyway because they are in a hurry to get back to work.

Realistic expectations are hard to build, and political correctness makes it harder. It trains you to feel guilty about focusing on your own needs. It suggests you are a helpless victim of injustice, which undermines your confidence in your own steps. When you feel helpless, addiction may seem like a reasonable alternative.

Addiction triggers dopamine by creating the illusion that you are meeting a need. Whether you are addicted to a substance or a behavior, that first surge of dopamine built a pathway that triggers more good feelings when you think about getting more. Each step toward more triggers more dopamine. Every brain seeks dopamine, but if you seek it in ways that undermine your ability to meet your needs, you're in trouble.

Addictions are widely blamed on our society. This further reinforces the belief that you are powerlessness over your brain. The alternative is to understand that our brains are not designed to release dopamine for no reason. The good feeling is meant to flow when you approach a reward that meets a need. Social needs are important once physical needs are met, but the brain habituates to social rewards the way it habituates to physical rewards.

Political correctness is a kind of addiction. It stimulates the feeling of approaching rewards in the short run, though it hurts more than it helps in the long run. Fantasies about altruism can stimulate dopamine because you anticipate a social reward. But even that can't trigger it constantly. If you believe others get it constantly, you feel deprived. You blame injustice. Why wouldn't you? Everyone else seems to think this way.

Political correctness cultivates your sense of grievance by asserting that others get more rewards with less effort. It floods you with data to prove this, so it's hard to think otherwise. It tells you that your quest for rewards is hopeless, so you are motivated to focus on politically correct quests rather than your own. So you end up investing your energy helping the gatekeepers of political correctness get rewards rather than yourself.

10.
The mammalian urge for social dominance

The animal brain cares about social dominance because that promotes survival. An animal gets bitten or clawed if it reaches for a resource near a bigger critter. It avoids conflict in order to survive. But it still needs to eat, so it looks for a place where it can be in the one-up position. Serotonin is released when a mammal gains the one-up position. The good feeling tells you it's safe to assert yourself to meet your needs. You may find it hard to think of our furry friends in this way, but dominance behavior has been widely studied.

We have inherited a brain that rewards you with a good feeling when you come out on top. No one likes to admit to the pleasure they take in social dominance, though we easily see this in others. The point is not that we *should* dominate others to feel good; the point is that we do; and if we ignore our own urge for serotonin, we believe others are tying to dominate us.

When an animal finds itself in the one-down position, its brain releases cortisol and it retreats. That promotes survival, despite missing out on some food or mating opportunity, because the critter stays alive to eat or mate another day. Mammals survive by constantly scanning for opportunity to be in the position of strength. The mammal brain is always comparing itself to others and judging its strength relative those around it. Social comparison is more primal than food and sex in the sense that it always comes first.

Social comparison is more primal than food and sex because it always comes first.

This is why people are so relentlessly concerned with how they stack up against others. When you find yourself in the one-down position, cortisol can make you feel urgently threatened. That makes it easy to believe a grave injustice has been done. It's harder to believe that you are just trying to stimulate your serotonin, and so is everyone else.

Neurons connect when serotonin flows, so each brain learns to expect it in ways that stimulated it before. The one-up experiences of your past wired you to seek good feelings from similar situations today. Your one-down experiences wired you to expect bad feelings in similar settings. We all see the world through the lens of our old serotonin circuits.

Serotonin is not aggression; it's calm confidence in your ability to meet needs in the face of rivals. We have many names for this feeling: pride, status, power, ego, recognition, appreciation, control, social importance, getting respect, feeling special. We use negative words when our rivals seek it, and positive words when we seek it ourselves. We don't notice that it's the same feeling.

Serotonin is quickly metabolized so the good feeling is soon gone. After all you did to trigger it, now you have to find another way to stimulate it. Serotonin did not evolve to flow all the time; it evolved to motivate survival behavior. If you released it all the time, you might put yourself above others in ways that threaten your survival. You might erode social bonds and lose out on oxytocin. You could get yourself killed. This is why our brain carefully chooses its serotonin opportunities.

Dominance behaviors evolved because they reduce the conflict of living in groups. You might think it's the opposite until you see it from an animal perspective. When a social animal sees a reward, a group mate sees it too. If both lunged at it, one of them would get hurt. The weaker individual would get hurt, so natural selection built a brain that compares itself to others and informs you neurochemically to avoid harm on the path to rewards. This is why your brain is so busily comparing, despite your best intent.

In the modern world, we do not bite or claw our way to food and mates, but we are keenly sensitive to social rivalry. You worry about losing rewards to others, and your mammalian neurochemicals make it feel like your life depends on it. It can feel like a fight for crusts of bread in a concentration camp, even in the midst of a comfortable life. Anyone who stands between you and a resource triggers your threat chemicals, even if you don't see yourself as "that kind"of person." If the object of your affection smiles at someone else, your mammal brain fears the annihilation of your genes though you would never consciously think that.

When the one-up position is finally yours, it seems only fair. You don't think of yourself as greedy or selfish the way "they" are. You are just trying to survive.

It's natural to *want* the good feeling of serotonin all the time. And now we are trained to believe that we *should* have it, we *can* have it, that everyone else is having it, and thus we are wrongly deprived if we don't. This unmet need commands our attention when other needs are met, so in the midst of a life with more comfort and freedom than your ancestors' wildest imaginings, you can perceive your life as traumatic.

Political correctness amplifies this feeling. It suggests that "they" are putting you down and stealing your happiness. It trains you to believe that a few powerful individuals strut around feeling good all the time, thus depriving everyone else. It alarms you with endless messages about the dominators who want to crush you. This belief gets so deeply wired in that it's hard to see otherwise.

Political correctness has strict prescriptions about who should be one up and who should be one down. It commands many people to put themselves down, but it offers a compensating way to be one-up: by accusing others of insensitivity. This immediately puts you above them. You can enjoy a sense of social dominance by imaging the deplorability of others, and when the serotonin passes, you can imagine that again.

When you condemn others for racism, sexism, and other thought crimes, you're rewarded with a feeling of moral superiority. Your political correctness is evidence that you are more loving and caring than others. It's a reliable way to feel more-than in a world that bombards you with chances to feel less-than. Your mammalian social-comparison impulse can go into overdrive in our hyper-connected media-driven world, but you can always comfort yourself with the thought that you are more tolerant and humble than those "jerks."

You're rewarded with a feeling of moral superiority when you condemn others for racism, sexism, insensitivity, and other thought crimes.

Being offended is another politically correct way to be on top. The person you accuse of offense must now humble themselves to atone. It's easy to gain the one-up position this way because we're all guilty until proven innocent in the world of political correctness.

The ultimate serotonin booster is to condemn everyone in a position of authority. When you say "they're all a bunch of crooks," you put the high and mighty below you. Political correctness tells you that you're changing the course of history, so it makes you as powerful as any historical figure without leaving your couch.

The ultimate serotonin booster is to condemn everyone in a position of authority.

It's unpleasant to seek social dominance the old-fashioned way is. Brawling mano-a-mano like our ancestors is not appealing. Working your way up the career ladder with years of effort is unpredictable and un-fun. So it's tempting to stimulate your serotonin by putting down anyone who seems to be in authority. The gatekeepers of political correctness provide you with a constant stream of support for that.

But you pay a high price for politically correct serotonin strategies because you must subordinate yourself to the gatekeepers first. You must put down your society, your culture and yourself to have the new society that promises to put you on top.

Many people do submit because serotonin is so hard to sustain in other ways. You don't consciously think of political correctness as a serotonin strategy. You believe you are just standing up for the little guy in a cruel world. This seems so obvious that you don't think of it as a construction of your own brain. It's important to know more about the animal brain's quest for social dominance.

A reptile literally compares itself to everything that moves. It runs if it sees that it's smaller than the creature next to it. If a reptile sees that it's bigger, it tries to eat the other. And if it's about the same size, it tries to mate it. The mammal brain processes more detail than that, but it still boils it down to the same choice between confidence or threat.

Herd animals feel threatened when they're at the edge of the herd, so they push toward the center with whatever strength they have. After a lifetime of pushing, a critter is too weak to prevail and ends up around the edges. There it is likely to get picked off by predators, but if it's lucky, it has already raised its child on the inside. I explained these facts of life to my son, and he said the old mammals sacrifice themselves for the greater good. This is not actually how the brain works, of course, but the truth was too awful for my son to accept. He would be ostracized from the good-guy herd if he deviated from the altruism myth, and that would threaten my genes, so I let it be. Of course I am not saying we *should* spend our lives pushing our way to the center. I am saying we must recognize our own urge to push or we waste our lives feeling victimized by the pushing of others.

With more neurons we get more subtle conflict instead of outright pushing. Chimpanzees have more neurons than other mammals except humans, so their rivalries help us understand the life-and-death feelings we have over small perceived slights. Male chimps compete for reproductive opportunity in a fascinating way. They are only interested in females who are actively fertile, and that only happens about once in five years. (It takes that long to gestate and lactate each child.) When opportunity finally arrives, stronger males restrict the access of weaker males. So a male can spend years striving to advance in the male hierarchy just to be there at the right moment. A social hierarchy emerges organically as each chimp tests its strength against others.

Female chimps are as hierarchical as the males. When a group of ladies goes out foraging, the dominant lady commands the best spot in front of the choicest food. The others array themselves around her in order of social dominance. The weakest lady may find herself at a spot with less food and more exposure to predators. Each chimp is highly motivated to raise their status because brains that did that survived. I am not saying we should struggle to command the best spot. I am saying we should take responsibility for our impulses instead of blaming them on "our society."

You have probably heard that bonobos are different. They are known for having sexual contact with anyone at any time. The facts are more complicated. Bonobos use sexual contact to ease conflict with stronger individuals. We should not confuse this with "love." If you have to pleasure a stronger group mate to prevent them from biting you, it's the opposite of love.

Mammals have social hierarchies because each brain remembers its strength relative to others. The mammal brain links each group mate to either serotonin or cortisol, which prompts either assertion or withdrawal. A young mammal builds these circuits during interactions that humans call "play." When you see young animals "playing," they are testing their strength against others, and feeling good or bad about the results. This builds the circuits that help them assert for resources while avoiding conflict.

Most mammals have dominance-submission rituals to prevent conflict. This clarifies the relative status of two mammals as soon as they meet. The one who perceives itself to be in the position of strength makes a dominance gesture. The other responds with a submission gesture, unless they see themselves as stronger. Submission protects you from attack, but you miss out on serotonin and any resource at stake. Fights only erupt when both individuals perceive themselves to be the likely winner. Most of the time, one individual backs down to protect itself from harm.

Dominance rituals get the uncomfortable business of status out of the way, allowing group mates to get on cordially. The serotonin relaxes the dominant individual, which reduces its aggression. Self-protective caution restrains the weaker individual. Any resources that present themselves are understood to belong to the stronger individual, but if a predator strikes, the stronger will take risks to protect the weaker. Relative strength may change over time, and new hierarchies emerge.

The point is not that we *should* create social hierarchies. The point is that we do, and instead of blaming it on others we can recognize our own active role. When you see how your brain creates this drama, you have more power over the impulse. You may feel one-down when you see others having more nuts than you. You can improve your nut-cracking skills, or you can find other ways to one-up them. Political correctness trains you to focus on the latter.

Nuts are so hard for a monkey to crack that they often live with failure. They watch others enjoy nuts while they have none. Most monkeys just keep trying, but some turn to bullying. Political correctness is like bullying. You accuse others of an ism in order to get their nuts. You can say they are the bully you, and ignore the fact that you are the one who is threatening and demanding resources from them. They may give you the resources because they would rather invest their effort in nut-cracking than in fighting you. Our brain is constantly learning from rewards. If bullying gets rewards, a brain wires itself to go there instead of building other skills.

If bullying gets rewards, a brain wires itself to go there instead of building other skills.

Everyone has had childhood experience with being one-down in some way. Money and grades are obvious measures, but more personal factors are often involved. Maybe you had a cruel sibling or a cousin who always seemed a step ahead. Cortisol built a pathway that inclines you to feel one down today. Your brain easily finds facts that fit, so it always seems like everyone has more nuts than you. You deprive yourself of serotonin when you do this. That leaves you eager for other serotonin strategies, such as political correctness. You can always feel superior about your humility.

Your inner mammal thinks you will be happy all the time if only you can seize the one-up position from those who are depriving you. Of course we all know that doesn't work in practice. The tabloids make it clear that social importance does not bring lasting happiness. But your inner mammal still gets hooked when you fall short in your own social comparisons.

If you took off the deprivation goggles, you would see that we all have the same dilemma. No matter how many nuts you're born with, your brain takes what you have for granted and looks for ways to feel bigger and better. If you succeed, the good feeling is soon metabolized and you feel threatened until you can stimulate it again. The more nuts you have, the more you worry about losing them, as we'll see in the following chapter.

11.
The mammalian urge to avoid pain

Stress and pain are the same thing to the mammal brain. They're a a release of cortisol.

Cortisol is the body's emergency broadcast system. It makes you feel like something awful will happen if you don't make it stop. You need to know where the threat is coming from in order to make it stop. That's easier when it's a big surge from a big pain. But stress is a small drip of cortisol, so it's hard to know where it came from.

Political correctness offers a solution. It tells you that your stress is caused by "our system," and the way to relieve it is by fighting the system. That message is attractive to a stressed modern brain.

Avoiding pain is the top priority of a survival-focused brain. Animals are always avoiding pain. When they smell a predator, cortisol is released and they run. When their blood sugar falls, cortisol is released and they seek food. When they see a stronger group mate near the resource they're eyeing, cortisol is released and they restrain themselves.

Stopping cortisol is hard for the modern human brain. We trigger it by exposing ourselves to threat messages in the news. We worry about the long-run consequences of our short-run pleasures. We lie to ourselves about the source of our pain by saying "that doesn't bother me." So our cortisol keeps making us feel like something is urgently wrong.

Political correctness appeals to that something-is-wrong feeling. It helps you make sense of your cortisol with the simple assertion that "our society the problem." This is easy to believe because when you struggle to explain your threatened feelings. When you know how cortisol works, you can escape this belief.

Cortisol motivates a child to pull their hand off a hot stove without need to fully know what it means to get burned. Pain is a surge of cortisol that motivates immediate action. Neurons connect when cortisol flows, so the next time the child sees a hot stove, cortisol turns on sooner. Thus a child anticipates pain and acts to protect itself. Cortisol circuits last, so we can end up anticipating pain a lot. That's efficient in the state of nature, where fire is always hot and ice is always cold. But social pain complicates things.

Isolation equals pain from the mammal brain perspective because mammals are born helpless. They experience pain when no one is there to meet their needs. Cortisol wires a brain to feel threatened by separation from its source of support. This is an effective survival system in a world where social isolation can land you in the jaws of a predator in an instant. Each brain avoids the pain of social isolation with circuits built from its own life experience. A bad hair day can trigger your cortisol if it fits your early experience with social isolation.

Conflict is another cause of social pain. Social animals learn to avoid conflict to avoid pain. They are not motivated by abstractions about etiquette or ethics; they are motivated by visceral fear of bigger critters. Cortisol circuits motivate the self-restraint necessary to stay safe at close quarters with stronger individuals. Cortisol circuits motivate humans to honor their commitments and leave the last banana for others. But you may end up resenting the bananas of others, thus triggering internal conflict even you avoid external conflict.

To complicate life further, disappointment triggers cortisol. A hungry lion surges with cortisol when it sees its prey escape. The bad feeling motivates the lion to stop its chase, which saves its energy for a better prospect. Disappointment promotes survival because a lion would starve to death if it kept feeling good about a gazelle that got away. Disappointment helps a mammal avoid pain by discouraging ineffective efforts so we can shift to more effective ones.

If you expect a promotion or a party invitation that doesn't come, cortisol creates a bad feeling. It's not an immediate survival threat, but the cortisol of disappointment makes it feel that way.

Cortisol does its job by making you feel so bad that you can't focus on anything but escaping the threat. When a gazelle smells a predator, it would rather keep grazing but it runs because that relieves the cortisol. Hunger triggers cortisol, but the smell of a predator triggers more. A gazelle doesn't expect to eliminate bad feelings forever; it just focuses on the most immediate threat.

Humans can anticipate future threats. We prevent pain by to prevent it. But when we succeed, we scan for the next potential source of pain. Our brain is not designed to sit around and feel safe. It's designed to find the next most pressing threat. You can end up with that "do something!" feeling all the time, and no way to make it stop.

Distraction helps the human brain relieve threatened feelings. Distraction doesn't promote survival when you're actually chased by a predator, but when the threat is just electricity flowing through a neural pathway, you can relieve it by sending electricity into a different pathway. Political correctness helps you do that. It shifts your attention from up-close personal threats to distant abstract threats. When you're afraid to stand up to a real person in your life, it feels good to rage at a leader on a screen. They cannot retaliate.

When a baboon is threatened by a lion, it runs up a tree. The feeling of relief is so great that it wires the baboon to look for trees when it's threatened. Our brains are the same. Whatever relieves your threatened feelings promotes survival from your mammal brain's perspective, so you get wired to look for. If political correctness helps you escape threatened feelings, you look for that. For example, when you suffer a social disappointment, theories about injustice may give you a sense of relief. The good feeling of builds a pathway that lights up theories about injustice the next time you feel threatened. It feels absolutely true because your electricity flows so easily. You might turn to political correctness the way others turn to a cigarette.

Without political correctness, disappointments fill your mind with a sense of threat that you feel powerless to escape. You actually feel safer hearing the alarmist messages in "the news" because it distracts you from threats to yourself. You feel safer when you bond with those who share your sense of alarm. You feel safer when your skillful critique of "our society" raises your status. You would lose all that if you deviated from political correctness. Its seems too threatening to even consider.

And yet, it's hard not to question political correctness because you keep stumbling on experiences that conflict with it. You try to conform by blaming the designated bad guys, but you can see that it's more complicated. You see that designated good guys threaten you sometimes. You feel like a lamb being told to lie down with a lion.

Designated good guys threaten you sometimes. You feel like a lamb being told to lie down with a lion.

You avoid saying this, and even thinking it, because the prospect of social isolation is so painful. This double bind triggers lots of cortisol. You have learned to distract yourself from cortisol with theories of injustice, so you're in a loop.

You may pride yourself on independence. You may think you could not possibly be influenced by the fears of others. But in the state of nature, a critter who refused to run when its herd mates ran would get eaten. We are not descended from that critter. We inherited a brain that trusts the alarm calls of its mates. When everyone around you feels threatened by white supremacists, you are likely to feel it to.

Our ancestors didn't worry about distant threats because immediate threats were so pervasive. My mother grew up with actual hunger and violence in her home, which was the norm for many in human history. Today, most people grow up without such direct threats, which frees their natural alarm system to scan for more distant potential threats. Small social disappointments can feel like full emergencies when there's no wolf at your door. Nature's alarm system does not turn off when you have a comfortable life. It just widens its scope.

I contributed to this alarmism as a college professor (beyond my general negativity about "our society") in my lessons on "Total Quality Management." TQM tells you to treat every defect as a crisis. It brought great strides in quality by undoing the natural impulse to cover up defects. It grew from the policy of stopping the production line when a defect is discovered so engineers can gather data about its cause. TQM helps us reduce defects by tracing them and fixing them at their source. The sense of urgency about defects helped American companies compete with the rising quality of Japanese products. But TQM ushered in a culture that's always looking for defects and treating them as a crisis.

TQM's success in raising quality was barely noticed. Our cars rarely break down anymore, but instead of feeling good about it, we direct our sneering at new targets. Our brain doesn't waste bandwidth on things that go right.

Our natural impulse to anticipate and prevent threats has been intensified by lawsuits. When something goes wrong, we find someone to blame for having failed to anticipate and prevent it. This builds a constant fear of overlooking a preventive action and being blamed for it.

Fear seems weak, so many people cover their fear with anger, which seems strong. Anger is the urge to go toward a threat despite the natural impulse to run from it. Anger is rare in nature because running toward a threat rarely promotes survival. Animals only attack when escape is not possible, or when they have a clear advantage. Testosterone surges when attack is your best survival option. Political correctness advocates anger. It promotes the belief that you are cornered by a predator so attack is your best option.

Our ancestors used testosterone cautiously. The mammal brain is good at calculating when anger promotes survival and when it doesn't. For example, some baboons run when a lion approaches, while others get aggressive. The alpha of the troop fights, and that promotes his genes because he is the father of many of the young. Even if he dies, his genes will benefit. Other baboons benefit their genes by running away so they live to reproduce another day. Each brain interprets threats in a way that best meets its needs.

Getting angry at your boss or your family may not help you meet your needs. You can protect yourself by lashing out at our society instead. It feels good to rage at lobbyists, imperialists, and "the rich" for this reason. You get the good feeling of chasing away a predator without risking real conflict. Each time you do it, the joy of relief builds the circuit bigger.

Our biggest circuits are built from the stresses of our myelin years. Whatever caused you pain when you were under eight and during puberty built the pathways that turn on your cortisol today. It's easier to see this in others— try asking people about their early pain and compare that to their present pain. Just thinking about your youthful social threats can be painful because we experienced them with a vulnerable young limbic system rather than a leafy adult cortex. Your circuits were built by that vulnerable perspective, not from your present mature perspective. Understanding your early threat circuits helps you understand the threatened feelings you have today.

Beneath our individual differences, it's easy to see that each brain seeks social power, and feels threatened when its social power is threatened. We hate to acknowledge this, so it's useful to know that baboons spend a lot of their time gazing at higher-status individuals in their troop. Researchers have found that baboons will even exchange food for the opportunity to gaze at photos of their troop leaders. This is the monkey equivalent of buying tabloids, and it's eerily similar to the high school focus on "popularity."

Imagine a high school cafeteria where students focus their attention on a table of "popular" kids. That table has eight seats, so most kids are by definition "excluded." Your mammal brain perceives this as a threat, even if those kids did nothing to actually threaten you. It's easy to blame those feelings on others, and hard to acknowledge your own urge to sit at that table. This sense of grievance helps you bond with others who feel aggrieved. The bonds feel good, but since they're built on bad feelings, you have to keep feeling bad to enjoy them.

Mammals have always competed for status as if their lives depend on it. Human status was more rigid in the past, so you didn't necessarily aspire to advance and then get disappointed. Many barriers have fallen in the past century, so every child is now burdened with expectations of being a super star. Such expectations are fed by the adolescent longing for the respect of their peers. Few young people even went to high school a century ago, but today, most adolescents spend most of their lives surrounded by other adolescents. Sheltered from real threats by adults, social disappointments become huge threats in their minds.

Sheltered from real threats by adults, social disappointments become huge threats in their minds.

If you constantly perceive yourself in the one-down position, you are constantly restraining yourself with cortisol. Humans call this impulse "shame." You may not call it shame with your verbal brain, but you feel it with your neurochemical brain. It's easy to believe that others are intentionally shaming you.

Political correctness tells you that others are shaming you, and then trains you to rise up by shaming others. You can end up spending much of your life trying to shame others without knowing it.

Political correctness tells you that others are shaming you, and then trains you to rise up by shaming others.

Political correctness promises a utopia where you are in the one-up position all the time. This is so appealing that your mind goes there again and again. Repetition builds a neural pathway that believes political correctness will relieve pain for good. Facts that fits this pathway flow effortlessly from your senses to your brain, so you feel like it's a fact.

You may imagine animals living in such a utopia, so it's useful to take a closer look. When you see a lizard basking in the sun, you may think it's enjoying the peace that prevailed before "our society." But the truth is that lizards are constantly running from pain. A lizard can get eaten alive in an instant when it is out sunning. It would rather hide under a rock, but it gets cold there. That triggers cortisol, which tells the reptile to go out and sun itself. The exposure puts the reptile on high alert until it's warm enough to go back into hiding. A reptile spends its life running from pain.

We have inherited a brain designed to assess threats and act to prevent them. We often find ourselves with a sense of threat as a result. The urge to eliminate threats has been useful– humans babies are hardly ever eaten by lions. But our endless quest to anticipate threats is stressful. Political correctness feeds on that natural bias.

Political correctness constantly alarms you with hell-in-a-handbasket messages. It offers you relief, but threatens to increase your pain if you dare to question it. It's a two-edged sword that relieves stress in the a moment only to trigger more of it over time. This is the essence of addiction: immediate relief followed by unfortunate consequences, followed by another quest for immediate relief, and more unfortunate consequences.

12.
The mammalian urge to leave a legacy

Thinking about your legacy may seem pretentious, but your mammal brain goes there a lot. It rewards you with a good feeling when you do things that preserve your unique individual essence. And it alarms you with bad feelings when you see obstacles to your individual survival.

Animals are not consciously interested in their genes. They do things that keep their genes alive because natural selection built a brain that makes it feel good. For most of human history, your children were your legacy, and promoting the survival of your children and grandchildren made you feel good.

In the past, people taught their children to carry on their traditions and it eased their inner mammal's survival fears. In the modern world, few people get to see themselves in their grandchildren, for a wide range of reasons. This is why we're so eager for alternative ways of leaving a legacy.

"Changing the world" is one modern way to do that. Political correctness persuades you that you are changing the world, and it feels good.

The human brain's awareness of its own mortality creates our sense of urgency about the future. You know that your quest to survive will fail someday. Your cortex can construct thoughts that terrorize your mammal brain. Relief comes from finding a way to keep some part of yourself alive. Legacy-building was a powerful motivator throughout human history. People built monuments and pyramids. They produced art, music, and literature. They created organizations and inventions that survived. Even being a carpenter or a teacher allows something of yourself to survive. And before the era of birth control, children were the legacy that came easily to most people. Investing yourself in something that survives eases our natural survival fears.

But the more you seek comfort in a legacy, the more you feel threatened by threats to your legacy. This is why a rejection of your poetry feels like a survival threat. This is why you feel so threatened when someone messes with your special family recipe. We can't control what happens after we're gone, so we're eager for legacies we can control today.

Many people are eager to "save the world" today. It helps relieve that awful awareness of a future you will not be a part of. Each politically correct action helps you feel like you're shaping the course of history. It can help promote your poetry too, because running with a powerful herd improves prospects for your art, your carpentry, and even your children. Of course you don't mention that because acknowledging self-interest gets you banished from the herd.

The fleetingness of life is hard to make peace with. Our ancestors confronted death more viscerally because their loved ones died younger, at home, and without lab tests to predict the timing. Today, we try to avoid bleak realities by searching for a life with "meaning." It's not easy to define meaning in a way that banishes existential fears. It's tempting to let the gatekeepers of political correctness define it for you. Fighting "the power" is the preferred source of meaning in the communications professions, like media and education, so it's the meaning we hear most about.

But you pay a high price for the politically correct approach to legacy. Thou shalt not have other legacies. Political correctness berates other legacies, such as passing your grandparents' traditions on to your grandchildren. It requires you to believe that our culture is bad and must be eliminated. It deprives you of pride in your traditions unless you re-define them to fit the politically correct agenda. And even if you do have the pleasure of grandchildren, political correctness persuades you that their survival prospects are awful. Thus, politically correct action still feels like the only way to build a legacy.

Religion and financial accumulation are other traditional sources of comfort that political correctness disdains. The more comforts you eliminate, the more you need to change the world to feel good.

Political correctness addresses our natural anxiety about aging by redirecting it against "the system." It elicits fear of inadequate care in your final years, which distracts you from the inevitable end of that care. Your fears get channeled into fear of service cuts, so you feel like you're promoting your survival when you fight "right-wing threats" to your services.

Demanding more services feels so good that over-treated ends up being a threat for many people. Over-treatment is blamed on corporate greed because that is an acceptable bad guy, but a huge engine of over-treatment is political correctness. Its quest for "disparities" and big lawsuits in the name of the "little guy" motivate defensive treatment that does no good.

Over-treatment is paid for with debt that makes it harder for your offspring to survive. The debt incurred to pay for these services is your legacy to your grandchildren. The politically correct will shun you for saying that, however. To protect yourself from social isolation, you can never acknowledge the harm done by political correctness. You must blame all harm on "the system."

Curiously, animals build their legacy by fighting the power. But the energy they can spend doing this is limited because they have to spend so much energy just filling their bellies. Today you can have a lot of energy left. You don't have to plant or harvest or preserve food, or starve during dry seasons. Many people don't work or have children. A lot of primal energy is left to invest somewhere. You are celebrated as a good person if you invest it in "meaningful" projects as defined by political correctness. The result is a lot of primal energy available for fighting the system.

Part 3
Life without
Political Correctness

When I discovered my politically correct goggles I was eager to rip them off. I couldn't wait to see what life would look like without them. I thought it would be grand to see the world without preconceptions of victimhood.

But I soon found myself triggered by the swirl of politically correct conversations around me. I knew I was expected to agree but I didn't want to fake it. I realized that I needed to take some risk or I'd spend the rest of my life submitting to dogma that I didn't believe in. After learning so much about the mammal brain, I decided to meet my needs for social support, resources, and social significance without depending on political correctness. Here's how I did it.

I needed to take some risk or I'd spend the rest of my life submitting to dogma that I didn't believe in.

This is not a story of angry confrontation. I am not interested in fighting political correctness because most of my loved ones are among them. And I do not want a new embattled mindset after working so hard to shed the old one.

I do not want a new embattled mindset after working so hard to shed the old one.

Of course I am surrounded by the mammalian view that "if you're not with us, you're against us," so I may be the enemy in someone's eyes. It's worth the price to escape political correctness. But to keep the price as low as possible, I developed some practical guidelines.

1. I don't debate politics

Wars were fought to protect our freedom to discuss politics, but each time I hear someone chant the PC message of the day, I ask myself whether debating this particular individual is a good use of my time. Usually I decide that my time is better invested in another way.

If someone asks my opinion, I answer in a way that is honest but not derisive of others. I don't offer my opinion, and I don't offer my time to people who want to push their opinion on me. I am not against political discussions in principle, but the discussions around me are based on rigid assumptions about good guys and bad guys that people are not willing to question. These discussions are reasonable efforts to meet mammalian needs, but they're not my way to meet my needs.

2. I don't get defensive

I do not apologize for my failure to observe the rituals of political correctness. But I don't jump to the conclusion that others are hostile toward me either. That would risking creating hostility that isn't there. If someone is indeed hostile, I do not escalate. Instead of taking it personally, I think of it as a mammalian dominance ritual for a different species.

I keep my airspace clear of hostility by finding a way to exit from hostile discussions. I could not keep my cool if I allowed in the steady stream of politically correct messaging. Asserting my power over my own airspace protects me from feeling assaulted by political correctness.

3. I focus on my own needs

No greater good is served by perennial outrage about the state of the world. I can do more good by staying out of the frenzy. When I feel pressured to join it, I ask myself how best to meet my needs. I introduce a non-PC idea if the risk is manageable.

My sixty-second rule has been very useful: when a conversation turns toward derision of "right-wingers,"

I give it sixty seconds. Sometimes it passes. If it doesn't, I either say something authentic or find an exit. This simple rule meets my need to feel free of negativity.

You will develop your own guidelines for navigating the rocks between social animal and authenticity. I hope my navigation story will help.

13.
Valuing Authenticity

Authenticity releases the tension created by squelching yourself. Self-squelching is necessary at times for social animals, so each moment of authenticity is precious.

Valuing authenticity transformed my life. It focused me on what I had to gain so I didn't just worry about what I had to lose. I knew how to escape political correctness when I started valuing authenticity.

Being authentic doesn't mean telling others what they should think. It means deciding consciously when to conform instead of doing it automatically. Conformity is necessary sometimes, but you can expand your maneuvering room to get more of what you want without it.

We social animals make constant trade-offs between honoring our own impulses and honoring others. We squelch ourselves sometimes to avoid pain in the short run. But it's useful to be aware of the long-run cost of self-squelching. It burdens your body with real physical tension. I grew up squelching and it took me a long time to understand the cost.

There is no simple solution. Leaving the herd has a cost, but following the herd has a cost too. Ideally we can be individuals even while in a group. But in practice, the group feels threatened if you refuse to mirror them. They blame you for threatening them, so you may go along to relieve the tension. You end up with a lot of tension in the long run when you conform to escape tension in the short-run.

I decided to release that tension a bit at a time instead of letting it build. Each time I express my true thoughts, I'm rewarded with a small release. Of course it seems risky to reveal my true thoughts, but the long-run gain is worth a prudent risk.

My transition from political correctness happened without drama when I started valuing authenticity. No one cut me off in an acrimonious rage. Some falling-outs occurred but it was a mutual lack of effort. Some people lost interest in me when I failed to "empathize" with their outrage. I did not directly offend them, but I did not try to hold on to them by pretending to agree. From this middle ground, I let the chips fall where they may instead of expecting to control things.

Political correctness often tells you that your authentic responses are bad and you should replace them with more enlightened responses. You are taught to distrust what you know with your own eyes an ears, and substitute the voice of political correctness. Negating your true thoughts puts you in the one-down position. You are disrespecting yourself when you conform to political correctness against your own best judgment. Your inner mammal lives in total submission and it feels bad.

Once I saw how I was submitting, I stopped. I would not give strangers the keys to my brain. I would not make my inner mammal feel endangered all the time by ignoring the experience it accumulated over a lifetime. As much as I feared the judgment of others, I realized that my own judgment matters more.

At first, I feared ridicule, shunning, and excommunication if my apostasy was noticed. I thought of authenticity as a social gaffe, so I blamed myself. But when I learned that authenticity has value, I had something to put on the other side of the ledger. Self-acceptance has benefits that offset the costs of renouncing political correctness.

You can reveal your true thoughts without explosive venting. Disagreement doesn't have to be confrontational or derisive. It can be a simple mention of a fact that no one dares to acknowledge. You may only get silence in response, but you will prove to yourself that independent truth is possible.

Let's be practical. Imagine I'm seated at a table with people who start venting hatred of right-wingers. I do not want to listen to it. What do I do?

Plan A was to politely express disagreement as long as it wouldn't ruin my career or my family. But I rarely did it because it never seemed worth the risk. I needed a better way to operationalize this. Here is Plan B.

First, I wait sixty seconds before doing anything. Tolerating their hypocritical hate for a minute is better than having a hair trigger. Sometimes the topic passes, and I try to practice mutual acceptance instead of carrying resentment. If the topic continues, I have to make a choice. I developed a sliding scale to accommodate different risk scenarios.

The least risky option is to go to the bathroom. Sometimes it works! Either the subject passes, or people get the message that I don't share their views. That can be risky too, but it's better than open conflict.

But often I come back from the bathroom and people are still singing the politically correct opera. Then I might remember a dentist appointment. This might upset people who are expecting a sing-a-long, but it's worth the price to liberate myself from the expected submission.

Another option is to actively change the subject. This honors the person's effort to connect with me while freeing me from their political anger. When you change the subject, you may find that the other person is glad to talk about something other than politics. Where I live, expressing hatred of conservatives is like talking about the weather- it's just a ritual for seeking common ground. I can offer alternative common ground.

Where I live, expressing hatred of conservatives is like talking about the weather- just a ritual for seeking common ground. I can offer alternative common ground.

What if the person keeps bringing up politics and disappearing is not possible? Then I have learned to say "I don't think about it that way." I disagree without debating. This is a big change from my academic training, where you always justify your assertions with three pieces of evidence. In ordinary conversation that's not necessary. You just say you don't agree and wait to see if there's interest in more. If not, I can feel good about enjoying a moment of authenticity without violating the comfort zone of others. They miss out on the benefits of my wisdom, alas, and they may say I'm a Nazi behind my back. But I don't need to win everyone's approval or rescue the galaxy; I only need to make peace with my inner mammal.

You may imagine the uncomfortable silence after I disagree. It's natural to anticipate hostility during the silence, and it's tempting to fill in with my stockpile of wrath at political correctness. But that would not meet my needs. Instead, I respond to the silence with a personal anecdote that explains my disagreement. A personal story is less confrontational than a political statement. I could still end up with a worst-case scenario, but I don't torture myself with that thought. I focus on the best-case scenario: that silence means they fear incorrectness as I once did, and I am helping to build their tolerance for diverse views with my brief, relaxed comment. Maybe not now, but eventually.

Sometimes I risk a full debate. I rarely do it because it obliges me to listen as much as I speak. I hate listening to the same intellectual cliches I have heard all my life. So as soon as I see that the debate is not likely to be interesting, I stop speaking.

When I do debate, I have learned to do it without anger. At first, you risk spewing a lifetime of resentment onto the unfortunate person in front of you. But with practice, I learned to focus on the reward (authenticity) rather than the threat, so I don't feel angry.

At first, you risk spewing a lifetime of resentment onto the unfortunate person in front of you. But with practice, I learned to focus on the authenticity reward rather than the threat, so I don't feel angry.

What if someone does attack?

It only happened to me twice, once in person and once online. Both times it was people who have raged at plenty of others. In the online case, I was cordial but the person got nastier so I learned to say nothing. In the personal case, I was shocked to hear myself raging back at them. It taught me how to avoid escalating. I just remind myself that I am safe, so a dominance display is not necessary, even if the other person thinks they need to make a dominance display.

I don't go around expecting to be attacked. I don't attack others so they have no reason to attack me. And I don't easily interpret a statement as an attack. If I start to feel attacked, I wait sixty seconds, and then move up or down on the sliding scale. Usually I slide down and escape the conversation because I have wasted enough of my life on what I call the "freshman dorm conversation." I don't need to hear another sanctimonious recitation of PC pieties. I don't need to help other people process their anger. Occasionally I slide up and briefly explain my perspective. I keep it short so my obligation to listen is short.

We mammals naturally seek respect. The person I am debating with wants my respect. If I don't feel it, I fake it. But I don't want to spend my life faking things., so I minimize the encounter. Of course, that ends my opportunity to get respect from them. They may even disrespect me for my failure to embrace their enlightened views. But learning about my inner mammal taught me not to believe that my survival is threatened when I'm not in the one-up position.

The biggest challenge for me is people who pretend to be Socratic. They ask me questions, but they're not authentic questions. They say: "don't you think....?" But they have no interest in what I think. I politely say, "no I don't think that, because..." and they respond, *"but don't you think...."* They seem confused, as if no one has ever disagreed with their platitudes. That is the PC sport– shaming deviants into making profuse apologies. I do not let them shame me. I answer with my own views instead of kowtowing to the dogma. Usually the person gets bored after a few rounds. I get bored too. In the end, I can't control whether they excommunicate me. But I can feel good about nurturing my authenticity. Getting along with people has value, but authenticity has value too. If I expected myself to conform to a world view that seems false to me, I'd be endlessly squelched.

That is the PC sport–
shaming deviants into making
profuse apologies.

It feels unfair that I have to worry about offending people who are not worried about offending me. But I remind myself that they are paying a price for their conformity. We all face the same hard choices. I can't blame others for submitting because I did that when it met my needs. I understand their fear of being sneered at or hated. Political correctness is effectively their religion, and you can't expect someone to disavow their religion in a casual chat. Someday they may have a moment of insight the way I did.

My simplest solution is still my favorite: I go to the bathroom when a conversation turns to hating

Republicans. This protects me from getting triggered by a topic that may soon blow over. If the topic is still on when I get back from the bathroom, I look down instead of making eye contact. Usually the fire burns out. If not, this may not be the group for me. But sometimes people graciously accommodate me. In one group there was conscious agreement to avoid divisive topics, and in others it happened without explicit discussion. I could not have enjoyed this great outcome if I had just quit instead of being authentic. And sometimes I did quit because there was too little common ground.

It feels unfair that I have to worry about offending people who are not worried about offending me.
But sometimes people graciously accommodate me. I could not have enjoyed this great outcome if I had just quit instead of being authentic.

Small triumphs of authenticity were not enough, alas. I felt like something was missing: the oxytocin pleasure of trusting another human being. I longed to share my unfettered thoughts with other politically incorrect people. But I didn't know any, and after all my years of indoctrination, I was almost afraid of catching a social disease from them. The irony of having been trained by "liberals" to hate people I didn't know was not lost on me.

A bigger complication was my fear that new people would expect me to embrace their ideology just as the old people did. I knew I wouldn't follow a new herd, so I risked being snubbed yet again.

I lived in this limbo for a decade. If conservatives had horns, it would have been easier for me to find one to talk to. Then one day I stumbles on an ad for a conservative comedian hosted by the Republican Jewish Coalition. Wow. This had my name on it. I used to love comedy, and mourned the takeover of comedy by political correctness. I was eager to meet Jews with the courage to be openly Republican. So I went.

How do you to introduce yourself to people you've been trained to hate? You expect them to hate you, so you feel defensive. But I knew that my old impulses were misguided and was eager to feed my brain with new inputs. I even asked a question at the Q&A. I vividly remember because it was the day my baby was accepted into an especially left-wing university, and I was looking for support. (He went elsewhere, because of geographical amenities.)

In the end, I learned to think of people as individuals instead of as herd members. As much as

I'd love to have a herd that agrees with me on everything, I know that's just my mammal brain rather than a realistic expectation about human life. We humans are individuals because we wire our brains from life experience. Individual moments of authentic trust feel better than life in a herd unified by a common enemy. I can accept my mammalian nature without submitting to it.

I used to think other people enjoyed social trust all the time and I was missing out. But I realized that everyone has the same conflict between their primal urge for safety in numbers and their quest for authenticity. Infants seek perfect trust because they're so vulnerable. Adolescents do too. But as we mature, we can build more realistic expectations. We can find better ways to satisfy those life-or-death feelings about social trust. We can even enjoy moments of authentic trust with people who disagree with us.

The people around me may not think this way. They may even think I'm evil. But they are mammals seeking shared moments of authenticity too. I won't know where I can find it unless I try. We must risk the pain of rejection to reap the rewards of authenticity. Rejection is un-fun. Some people think it's better to cut someone off than to risk being cut off by them. But I did not want to add to the partisan polarizing by cutting people off. Rejection is easier to live with when you see yourself as a mammal rather than a victim.

I put more effort into people who are less political. In my world, that means people who don't bring up their hatred of right-wingers very often. When they do, my sixty-second rule goes into effect. If they keep bringing up politics, I will "come out" to the person and tell them I disagree with popular views of good guys and bad guys. Then they can decide how "tolerant" they are— unless it is my dentist, my haircutter, or my carpool driver, in which case I prefer that they stay calm.

I don't flood people with too much information. I just tell them that my life experience conflicts with the popular view of good guys and bad guys. Then I stop and listen. It's like having "the sex talk" with children — you focus on their questions instead of lecturing. Often I get no questions, but I tell myself that the person appreciates my trust anyway. I suspect they too are longing to escape political correctness, but fear being condemned by everyone they know. I don't need them to openly agree. I feel satisfied just by escaping another round of partisan finger pointing.

If the relationship survives and the person keeps offering political opinions, then I offer mine. I keep it short. It would be nice to be surrounded by people who agree with me on everything, but that doesn't happen naturally; it only happens when you live inside an ideological bubble with enforced conformity. For me, the self-squelching is not worth it. We do not need unanimity to survive.

We are always making decisions about how to spend our limited time on earth. We can spend it making others feel good in ways that leave us feeling bad, or we can choose different.

It would be nice to have people who always agree with me, but that only happens inside an ideological bubble with enforced conformity.

My authenticity has cost me at times. I used to reproach myself for that, but I keep reminding myself of the benefits that go with the costs. Maybe I saved myself from interactions that would have driven me nuts. Maybe I prevented a chronic illness by releasing tension. Maybe I opened a space that will be filled by something better. And maybe the costs would have happened even without my political incorrectness.

Authenticity is risky, to be sure. You can be accused of offending someone, and your side of the story may be ignored. Your character may be attacked and your cortisol may surge. But authenticity still has value. If someone thinks I must invest my energy in their cause, I don't have to agree. If this upsets them, I don't have to let it upset me. If the person gets aggressive, I can feel good about my self-protective skills. I will not aggravate things by anticipating aggression, however. And I do not feel trapped because my sliding scale gives me maneuvering room.

I have learned to give myself respect instead of waiting for the world to give it to me. I respect myself for choices that contribute to my a long-run health.

Long ago, a politically correct friend made an incorrect comment that has stuck with me. When I remarked on some injustice, he said "unfair, unfair, unfair, everything is unfair." I was shocked at the time. I had never heard anyone refuse to "empathize" with a grievance. Though I said nothing, the comment opened my eyes to the possibility of distancing from politically correct grievances. I remembered his authenticity years later when I noticed my self-squelching. And it taught me that our words can plant seeds in people's minds that sprout years later.

It takes a lot of self-restraint to live harmoniously with other mammals. But I need to build my own controller instead of letting the gatekeepers of political correctness theirs in me. Fortunately, that is the job my brain is designed for.

I need my own filter instead of the one installed by the gate-keepers of political correctness.

14.
How to be a good person
without Political Correctness

What it means to be a good person is defined by political correctness for most people these days. You're defined as compassionate and intelligent if you rant about injustice. If you don't, you're dismissed as a dumb narcissist. It's hard to feel like a good person when the culture defines you as bad.

But I don't see the virtue in political correctness. It focuses on self-serving goals. It trains people to feel oppressed instead of taking responsibility for their lives. It prevails through attack. It hurts people it purports to help. I would rather define "good" for myself.

You may ask how I can be a good person without sensitivity to the plight of the oppressed. It's because I know the long history of violence and conflict. I know that it's more complicated than the simple victim stories we are told. In real life, the good guys are not all good, and the bad guys are not all bad. We are being manipulated into getting angry at designated enemies by power-seekers striving to compete with other power-seekers. The greater good is not served by my anger, so I won't waste my life being angry.

I developed a plan to feel good without submitting to political correctness. First, I defined my own way of contributing to the greater good, and then I surrounded myself with supportive messages instead of politically correct messages. You may think this means living in a bubble, but I was already in the politically correct bubble, so alternatives were most welcome.

My contribution to the greater good is to create tools that help people manage their mammal brain. I give these tools away for free or at very little cost. I make them as useful as I can instead of just telling people what they want to hear.

You can find a way to contribute your skills to the greater good. Define it yourself instead of getting sidetracked by popular definitions of public service. Many things done in the name of "help" do not help. They often make things worse because they reward bad behavior. If you particpate, you are increasing bad just to be seen as good. You can do more good by disengaging from counter-productive trends, even if it gets you called a bad person.

When I was tempted to conform to the accepted view of a good person, I reminded myself of all the reasons that political correctness does not serve a higher purpose.

No greater good is served by training people to believe they are not responsible for whatever happens to them.

No greater good is served by teaching people to focus on injustice and ignore all the goodwill around them.

No greater good is served by reflexively hating everyone you think is more "privileged" than you are.

No greater good is served by raising children to believe they are helpless victims of a bad system.

No good is served by alliances with violent individuals just because you share a common "enemy."

No good is served by excommunicating people who don't vote your way.

No good is served by championing teen parenthood, since early deficits in brain development cannot be made up.

No good is served by making everyone guilty until proven innocent of preconceived injustices, and supporting accusers regardless of facts.

No good is served by raising children with the "if it feels good, do it" philosophy, and then blaming the system when you get bad results.

No good is served by teaching people to believe that all their problems are caused by right-wingers and must be fixed by fighting by right-wingers.

No good is served by teaching people that all their problems are caused by right-wingers & will be fixed by fighting by right-wingers.

Even with this clarity, my world was so saturated by politically correct bitterness that I felt bad whenever I let it in. So I decided to filter it out. This is a huge lifestyle step, but well worth it. I cannot control the world but I can control its access to my brain. Here's how I put that into practice.

I decided to filter it out.
I cannot control the world but
I can control access to my brain.

First, I ignore the news. It robs me of the peace I need to make a useful contribution. I read books (and listen to audiobooks) instead, and if anyone thinks I'm a bad person because I don't know the latest drama, it's a price I'm willing to pay.

Ignoring the news does not mean putting your head in the sand. It means freeing yourself from the artificial sense of crisis so you can decide for yourself what merits your attention. The news lures you with the promise of helping the little guys fight the big guys. You enjoy oxytocin as you bond with millions through the news. You enjoy dopamine as you anticipate the next episode in each crisis. Most important, you enjoy serotonin when you feel superior by knowing what's in the news. I learned other ways to stimulate these happy chemicals so I didn't have to rely on the news.

My "good" education taught me that following the news is a contribution to the greater good. Anyone who doesn't is thought of as shirking their duty to help fight the bad guys. But I see how the news is designed to heighten anxiety about a common enemy in order to solidify the herd. I don't want to spend my life fighting enemies defined by the people who make the news. I can find other ways to be a good, smart and caring person.

It took effort to strip the news from my life because it kept creeping in unbidden. My phone flashed headlines about the enemies of political correctness and I'd get get sucked in, so I found the setting to turn off those headlines. My web searches often lead to news sites with sidebars full of political correctness, so I trained myself not to look at the sidebars. I even asked my dentist to turn off the CNN monitor in front of me. You could say I would rather have my teeth drilled than listen to a tirade of political correctness.

I noticed how much progress I'd made one day when CNN was forced on me. I was boarding a plane and the line got held up while I was next to a monitor. I couldn't leave the line so I had to let it blast me for five minutes. I noticed how agitated it made me, and remembered that I used to feel that way a lot. I almost forgot what it was like, and realized that this is how most people feel all the time.

The urge to watch leaders in the news is easy to understand. Baboons spend a lot of time watching their troop leaders. The mammal brain evolved to monitor more powerful individuals, and seek their protection. In childhood, we got protection from people who disappointed us at times, so anger at our protectors got wired in. In adolescence, we shifted our attention to new leaders, and sometimes got angry at them. Anger gets rewards sometimes, and the brain repeats what gets rewarded. It's easy to see why people focus on the political soap opera, as bad as it feels.

Of course I want information about the world around me, so I looked for better sources. For example:

- I read a lot of science history. It's a fabulous window into how the world works. I have to credit my husband for this discovery, since it was the audiobook category we could best agree on for long car rides.

- I scan the listings of BookTV every weekend. It's sponsored by C-SPAN, so most of its offerings fit a partisan template, but occasionally I find speakers that aren't just new wine in old bottles.

- I read history. Historians are partisan mammals, of course, but I look for older history books with something other than the same grievances in different costumes. I especially love reading the original journals of early travelers.

- I read biography, because every life story holds kernels of truth even though the author is a partisan human. Old biographies are a source of information that hasn't been filtered by new editors. New biographies are less interesting to me because they're so heavily drenched in preconceived beliefs about victimhood.

- I ignore best seller lists, and take recommendations from individuals who are not strong partisans. Then I spend time learning about the author and scanning readers' comments.

- I listen to audiobooks whenever I drive, exercise, or do housework. This dramatically increases my "reading" time.

- I read old books. Every time period has its own brand of political correctness, but opportunity for a fresh insight is higher among books that are not filtered by today's editorial and academic establishment. We are taught to condemn old books as racist, but I will not dismiss centuries of insight because the gatekeepers tell me to.

I used to love book stores, but I realized that I had to comb through ninety-nine politically correct books to find one with something else to say. That big PC blast was so unpleasant that I now do my browsing online. As soon as I see the "our society is the problem" message, I move on. It takes a big effort to find new insights that feel worth reading, so I have learned to enjoy the browsing instead of getting frustrated by it.

The same applies to my leisure time, which is stalked by PC messaging. I used to love theater, but now most plays have the same oppression theme. I used to love comedy, but that has gone the same way. I love historical walking tours when I travel, but these tours focus heavily on the oppression story so I feel like I'm hearing the same tour in every city.

Finding entertainment that doesn't bombard me with PC messaging is a huge challenge. I need down time like anyone, and do not want to spend it on yet another story of evil corporate titans getting trounced in the end by wiser, kinder poor people. I have to search hard for alternatives, so I do. I look for entertainment about the universal human condition with a note of optimism.

An interesting example is my local improv troop. They are the only comedy group I have found that finds humor in something other than ridiculing racists, sexists, and homophobes. Their characters resolve conflict by building trust instead of falling back on class warfare. I was so thrilled when I found it that I wondered how it happened. Alas, I made the uncomfortable discovery that the actors are PC in their private lives, and would rather be ridiculing racists, but they need to sell tickets to tourists to keep the theater alive, and the tourists include people they see as ignorant red-state racists. So instead of resorting to the same old tropes, they do amazing insightful comedy about the foibles that all humans have in common. Lucky me.

Our mammal brain fears social isolation so we fear being condemned as a bad person. But I didn't want to let fear define me. So I retrained my brain to hold onto my self-respect in a world that defines me as a racist-sexist-elitist-homophobic-Islamophobic-Nazi-hater-bigot. I learned to focus my attention on doing actual good instead of on winning the goodwill of the PC world.

15.
How to make a living without PC

No one wants to suffer a career setback from a wrong choice of words. Words are cheap, so people often say what it takes to protect their career prospects.

But after a while, it seems like nothing you say is enough. There is always another agenda that requires your support, and they want more than mere words. They expect you to put yourself down and put someone else up, regardless of the facts.

This frustration is amplified by our high expectations about job satisfaction, not to mention the real threat of financial insecurity.

Conforming at work triggers your cortisol, but the thought of not conforming triggers it too. It seems like there's no good alternative.

I lived with this conundrum for eight years, longing to escape the relentless dogmatism of my university, but knowing the value of my tenured position. Then on my forty-ninth birthday, I was surprised by an official notice from the State of California outlining the retirement benefits I would qualify for at age fifty. It wasn't much money since life expectancy at age fifty is so high, but it was a respectable exit strategy. I warmed up to the idea, and as my baby left for college, I became a Professor Emerita. I wasn't sure what I would do next, but I had a dream. I also felt like I had earned a little rest. When I left, no one cried.

Each of us confronts the workplace dilemma from the perspective of our unique individual circumstances. Here are my strategies for surviving the politically correct workplace that can fit into any life.

1. Live frugally

The less you spend, the less you need to do things just for the money. The more you save, the safer you feel when you risk authenticity. Frugality builds confidence in your ability to survive without pleasing politically correct gatekeepers.

I am not suggesting deprivation; I'm suggesting that your freedom expands with each purchase you resist. This is another ledger-balancing strategy to focus your mind on gains instead of losses.

Frugality only works if you are honest with yourself about the mammalian urge for social status. You may feel that people are judging your financial situation and your career success. But when you know your mammal brain, you know that you are making such judgments, about others and yourself. When you understand the animal urge for status, you can choose how you stimulate your serotonin instead of just depending on job status.

I wanted to give my children the best life possible, but my peace of mind could help them more than money. Quitting your job does not bring peace of mind, of course; you can end up in a psychological war with the world no matter what your employment status. I hoped to set my kids an example of calm, confident authenticity instead of being at war with the world.

Living frugally made escape an option, and that helped me stick it out another day, and another. Living frugally allowed me to write books I believe in instead of writing warm and fuzzy books about animal empathy. Living frugally helped me feel like I'm stepping toward a goal instead of feeling like a powerless victim.

I do not think people should quit their jobs to escape political correctness. I'm glad I stuck it out long enough to set an example of coexistence for my kids, who now have politically correct careers of their own. If everyone quit their politically correct job, it would just reinforce the belief that disagreement is not allowed. There is already an unfortunate effort to block the employment of people who question the politically correct agenda. Partisan polarizing will accelerate if no one challenges this effort. Living frugally strengthens your ability to challenge it.

2. Develop two hard skills

Hard skills make it easier to be judged by your work rather than by your loyalty to the politically correct agenda. Humans are inevitably political, alas. We are tempted to reward subjective loyalty more than objective contributions. But organizations need hard skills to survive, so they're your best shot at protecting your rewards.

Having two hard skills enables you to do things that few people can do. Find the overlap between the two skills and you are uniquely qualified for something. It might take some searching to find the role that requires both of your skills, but when you do, you become essential. You enjoy a bit of freedom. I am not saying you should use this freedom to be openly political at work, but when others are openly political, you have some alternative to slavish conformity.

Many of the hard skills are considered "boring." You may hate the idea of building one, no less two. We have been trained to believe that work should be "fun." We often hear interviews with successful people who say their work is so much fun that they would do it for free. Many people are persuaded that they should never have to do something un-fun, even expecting others to support them until they find work that's fun. This mindset doesn't prepare you for the real world, where getting along with others is never all fun.

If short-run fun is your standard of measure, building hard skills not appealing. If you were raised on PC messages about "passion," it takes some re-framing to focus on hard skills. All those people who say their work is fun are looking for the fun because they value work. They invent a lot of time in un-fun things before they get to the fun part. Hard skills can be boring at times, but a lifetime of political correctness is more boring, so it's nice to have a choice.

Fortunately, you can build hard skills in the context of something you already like. For example, I used my love of travel to build skills in the area of language, inter-cultural communication, and international finance. I used my love of reading to build skills in research and writing. You can find hard skills beyond programming and accounting, although these are excellent alternatives to political correctness.

Working with people who hate you for your political views is unpleasant, no matter how secure your income. But submission to an ideology is even more unpleasant. No matter how much you submit, you can lose it all by failing to submit to the next PC doctrine. Then you will wish you had hard skills, so you might as well build them now.

It's tempting to build a career by leveraging grievances instead. That strategy gets approval from teachers, journalists and politicians. People with hard skills are labelled "nerdy" because they are a threat to people who build their careers by exploiting grievances. But in adulthood you can transcend the circuits built from high-school shaming. You can get more rewards by finding things that need doing in the world, and do them.

3. Treat everyone with respect

You may find it irritating to pay taxes that support people who denigrate your work as complicity with "the system." Your frustration may build to the point where you vent it at politically correct office mates.

This is very bad for your survival, so it's essential to build a positive mindset about your PC co-workers.

People with hard skills are labelled "nerdy" because they are a threat to people who build their careers by exploiting grievances. In adulthood you can transcend the circuits built from high-school shaming.

Consider the possibility that they are stuck in the middle with you. This wonderful discovery is impossible if you look at them through the "us-vs-them" lens. Treat everyone with respect and you will slowly discover that many people are submitting to political correctness out of fear. They may not know it because they are not aware of their inner mammal. They are "useful idiots," in Lenin's parlance. Lenin built his revolution by provoking people to rage, rebel, and risk their lives; and then when he triumphed, he arrested the rebels and had them shot. Alpha gorillas do not like activists once they take power. You can take pleasure in your refusal to be a useful idiot, but you have to coexist with mammals who sacrifice themselves to the alpha.

Your coworkers may be imposing the "us-vs-them" lens on you, even though you have diligently resisted imposing it on them. You may think they are treating you as "the enemy." It's easy to fall into this perception because humans are indeed cliquey, political, competitive, and self-righteous. But if you automatically presume that you are being wronged, you have a victim mentality just as surely as if you were still politically correct. To escape political correctness, it's important to challenge those victim feelings with the historical perspective of mammalian social rivalry. The mammals you work with are looking for ways to one-up you, but if you get real you will see how you are doing the same. You will also see how they do it to people who share their politics. It's hard to sort out who does what to whom, so it's a waste of your energy to go there. Just respect everyone even though they are an irrational mammal.

When I started writing books, progress was slow and I was tempted to blame the "left-wing bias" of the publishing industry. I had to stop myself because I had blamed "right-wing bias" for the same dilemma just a few years earlier. I saw how easily the brain finds evidence to support its preconceptions. I decided to focus on my next step instead of on generalizations. I explained this to a friend, and she disagreed. She wanted me to blame the publishing industry, which in her opinion, really did change from a "right-wing" bias to a "left-wing" bias. She was trying to be helpful, but to me it didn't help. Blaming things out of your control brings relief in the short run but a sense of powerlessness in the long run. I decided to avoid such help.

If you are sure you are being mistreated because of your philosophical independence, seek legal remedies. Support is available from a variety of organizations that support civil rights in the true sense instead of in the usual good guys vs. bad-guys sense. But it bears repeating that you cannot vent your frustration with human irrationality at individuals. When political correctness gets on my nerves, I remind myself that it's my nerves, so I am responsible for managing them. I am less critical of my parents now that I understand how much strength it takes to pay the bills instead of exploding with frustration at the mammals you work with. Alas, they are gone.

If you are sure you are being mistreated because of your philosophical independence, seek legal remedies. But you cannot vent your frustration with human irrationality at individuals.

We mammals are ultra-sensitive about where we stand in the pecking order. Every group of mammals has its conventions about who must respect whom.

Political correctness is a new set of prescriptions about who submits to whom. It vents the inevitable frustrations of a group of competitive mammals by creating a new underclass: those who don't submit to its mandates. If you don't submit, everyone gets to disrespect you.

Political correctness is a new set of prescriptions about who submits to whom. It vents the inevitable frustrations of competitive mammals by creating a new underclass: those who don't submit to its mandates.

You have a right to your opinion in a democratic country, but those rights depend on the partisan humans enforcing them. You can lose your rights to anyone who says they are offended by you. Enforcers are tempted to defer to the angriest person just to protect themselves. Maintaining your rights takes some risk, but it helps you protect something more precious than your career: your ability to think for yourself.

When I took risks, I reminded myself that the potential consequences are mild compared to earlier periods of history. In Shakespeare's time, political incorrectness literally got your head chopped off. Other cultures have enforced conformity with other brutal execution methods, involving torture and cannibalism at times. This doesn't relieve the daily frustration of a politically correct workplace, but it frees you of the illusion that you chose the wrong job and a new job will fix it. People will still be mammals, and you will still be a mammal too. Mammals have always formed coalitions when it helps them compete, and turned on their allies when that advances them a bit more. So I stopped looking for the promised land and spend that energy focusing on my needs.

I used to feel deeply pained about my work being ignored, disrespected, and rejected. I felt unfairly deprived of the attention I deserved. Finally, I realized that everyone feels that way. So instead of feeling like something is wrong, I can just remind myself that we're all foraging for the next reward because our brain evolved to do that. If I see this as a crisis I will always be in crisis. I am better off accepting it. Now I can enjoy what I am working on instead of mourning the reward I woulda-coulda-shoulda gotten.

We mammals long for respect and attention, and resent others who seem to get more of it. We enjoy the spotlight because it stimulates our serotonin. From kindergarten birthday parties to high school cafeterias, we learn from whatever stimulates the good feeling, and then we try to stimulate it again. We get disappointed in our quest for serotonin, and we strive to avoid disappointment in the future. Managing your inner mammal is challenging, so it's good to know that everyone has the same challenge.

It's hard to keep showing respect where it is not reciprocated. You may feel a natural urge to retaliate despite the consequences for your livelihood. Animals resist put-downs to get food and mates, and we have inherited that urge to resist put-downs. When you feel put down by a coworker, they are probably not the real obstacle to meeting your survival needs. It helps to shift focus to more significant obstacles. Focus your power on your real needs instead of wasting it on anyone who plays a put-down game with you.

Political correctness is a massive put-down game. It asserts that everyone above you is there unjustly. Asserting yourself against them is a fast, easy way to raise yourself and stimulate serotonin. When the good feeling is metabolized, you can put them down again. You may not like it when others put you down, but the game sucks you in if you let it.

Political correctness is a massive put-down game. It asserts that everyone above you is there unjustly. It's a fast, easy way to enjoy serotonin, again and again.

For example, where I live, people hate those who drive big cars. They say big-car owners are putting us down, and they think they're opting out of the game by refusing to buy a big car. But their hatred for big-car owners means they're still in the game. They're still neurochemically responding to a status hierarchy defined by cars. They say this serves the greater good, but they are serving themselves by re-defining the hierarchy in a way that puts them on top. They applaud their superior values without seeing how these values leave them with constant hate.

We have inherited a brain that reacts to social status as if our survival depends on it. Whether you are highly ambitious or prefer a low-stress lifestyle, the people around you are keenly interested in their own social status. They have learned that political correctness is a convenient way to raise their status. If you don't join their team, they can raise their status at your expense.

The mammalian status game is frustrating, but it was frustrating before the age of political correctness. Instead of believing that your coworkers are putting you down, you can think of them as mammals trying to stimulate their happy chemicals. They are frustrated because the good feelings they expect don't always come, and when they do they don't last. They don't know why, and it's easy to blame others. They may even blame you if it helps them stimulate happy chemicals. You can find better ways to feel good instead of joining this game.

It's easier when you remember the zoological thought experiment. Every baboon is frustrated by the competition among troop its mates. It would rather seek greener pasture instead of tussling over the same dried-up patch. But as it distances from its support network, it feels threatened. Imagine a baboon who sticks with the troop until the the day it is gored by the canines of a bigger troop mate. It has had enough. It scuttles off despite the risk. Eventually it finds a new troop after a terrible time of hunger and fear. But the baboons in the new troop bare their teeth too. The mammal brain is remarkably consistent. Remember this when you long for a new group.

Work meets a wide range of needs in addition to the need for resources. It stimulates dopamine as you anticipate rewards for your efforts. It stimulates oxytocin as you give and receive support. It stimulates serotonin. when you enjoy a moment of social importance. But work is not a constant high of happy chemicals because they are soon metabolized. We always have to do more to get more. Our efforts to get them don't always succeed, and even when they succeed beyond your wildest expectations, the happy chemicals are soon processed and your brain looks for the next big thing. When you know how your own brain creates this frustration, your workplace feels less oppressive.

16.
How to enjoy social support without PC

For most of human history, people met their need for social support with enduring tribal bonds. Today, people often choose to leave old bonds and look for new ones. But new bonds are harder to create than we expect, so we often end up feeling threatened by social isolation. Political correctness can fill in the gap. It has become the glue that binds people in many places. Without political correctness, you are likely to be excluded by people who talk endlessly about "inclusion."

I did not want to get social support by faking beliefs I did not hold. After much trial and error, I learned to give my inner mammal the feeling of support without political correctness. Here are a few strategies.

1. Keep an open mind

People are quick to let you know how "progressive" they are where I live. They give you a progressive signal and expect you to respond with one. I don't give it, but I don't shut the door either. If I want acceptance, I must accept. So when people let me know how progressive they are, I see it as an effort to connect, and I offer an alternative way to connect. Sometimes it works; sometimes it doesn't; so I keep an open mind. And even when it doesn't work, I've have many positive experiences that started with a negative.

I don't harbor unrealistic fantasies, but I stay open to the unexpected.

2. The power of weak ties

We benefit from weak ties as well as strong ties. This point was made by a researcher who found that many jobs are obtained through weak ties. It wasn't influential close connections that mattered, but a large network of acquaintances that generated valuable information.

The theory of weak ties helped me feel good about the network I had instead of torturing myself with paranoid theories about an "old boy's network." Political correctness exaggerates the extent to which old boys help each other, and ignores the extent to which old boys undermine each other. Dramas about boarding schools make it clear why the old boys are in a hurry to get away from each other. It only seems like there's an old boy's network because mammals are good at forming temporary alliances to scratch each other's backs.

I built a large network of individuals who don't need to discuss politics. When people start complaining about "our society," I don't respond. Anyone who dislikes this need not be in my network.

3. I defined my needs carefully

Social bonds are usually sentimentalized, which obscures the role played by self-interest. Reciprocal obligation is the glue of mammalian social alliances.

More bonds means more obligation. This awareness freed me to make practical decisions about the bonds I really wanted. Sometimes I am seduced by the fantasy that other people are enjoying glorious social support and I am missing out. But then I come back to reality and notice that other people are choosing reciprocal obligations that work for them and I am choosing reciprocal obligations that work for me. People who seem to have an entourage of unconditional support are paying a price for it, and we are each deciding what price we will pay.

Each of us defines our social needs with circuits built from early experience. My experience is well described by an old Italian proverb: "better alone than in bad company" ("meglio soli che male accompagnati"). The social expectations we build in youth are deeply wired in. Re-wiring these circuits is possible, but only with a huge investment of effort. I decided to put my effort into the following item.

4. Don't take it personally

It's natural to feel bad if someone shuns you for political incorrectness, so I worked hard to re-wire this one. I started focusing on my choices instead of feeling wronged by other people's choices. I often choose not to support someone's victim story, so they have good reason not to build trust bonds with me. I can change that with a new choice if I want; but for now, I'm not the slightest bit interested in hearing more victim stories. So I focus on the benefits of my choice instead of the costs.

I don't rush to the conclusion that I am being shunned for political incorrectness. I stay open to every alternative. People have a right to seek social support in the way that is familiar to them. We are all making decisions about how to spend our limited energy. If my cortisol is triggered by a rejection, I don't go into a cortisol spiral. I respect other people's choices as well as my own.

5. Invest effort wisely

A smart person once told me that good relationships happen when you stop investing in bad relationships. She said you have to create a space before something comes to fill it. That gave me the courage to stop investing in people who would drop me in an instant if they knew that I didn't agree with their political correctness. I am creating a space. That space is scary unless you're creating it intentionally. Then, you don't know what will fill it, but you see it as a gain rather than a loss.

Of course I don't mean we should drop everyone we disagree with. I mean we should remember that our energy is limited and the more we invest it in bad relationships, the less we have for good relationships.

Baboons are always making decisions about whose fur they groom. They promote their own survival by seeking grooming partners who support them when threatened, or enhance their reproductive success.

This is hard to do. One grooming partner may disappoint, and another is so weak that their support is ineffective. Another embroils you in so many conflicts that the alliance hurts more than it helps. Baboons end up spending a lot of time grooming powerful individuals, in fact. They don't get a grooming in return, but they get a strong ally in future emergencies. It's like buying insurance. Political correctness is a way of grooming powerful allies, though no one likes to admit that. I have always preferred self-insurance. Instead of grooming powerful allies, I invest the energy in my own ability to manage future emergencies.

Of course I'm still a mammal so I need social support to feel safe. But I build realistic expectations about social support. I don't build idealized images of relationships that real life never lives up to. Political correctness trains people to expect utopian relationships, and bitterness results when reality falls short. Political correctness tells you to love everyone, and then it tells you to hate a lot of people. I would rather be honest about our mammalian nature. I can run my own social navigator instead of letting political correctness run it for me.

6. Invest in non-political social bonds

People who escape political correctness tend to have alternative support networks, like family and/or religion. Political correctness strives to sour you on family and religion, which makes it harder to leave. It's useful to build or restore alternative networks so you're not dependent on political correctness for social support.

For me, that includes something more subtle than family and religion. In my past life I was trained to sneer at "small talk." Only conversations about the awful state of the world were deemed worthy. Of course they always ended up in the usual critique of "our society." I do not want that bitterness and repetition in my life, so I had to retrain myself to be more open to "small talk."

Only conversations about the awful state of the world were deemed worthy. I do not want that bitterness, so I trained myself to be more open to "small talk."

Unfortunately, where I live, the political web encompasses everything. For example, if you joined an orchid society to talk about growing orchids, the conversation would soon turn to political enemies. So I have learned to be authentic before I invest too much. I do not flaunt my heresy with people I just met, but if they bring up politics, I say that I believe in the two party system and I'm uncomfortable with polarized partisanship. If I lose someone from saying that, it's worth the price. This was hard for me to do, but I was pleasantly rewarded with many apolitical conversations.

7. Get real about those adolescent circuits

You are "not cool" if you question the latest dictate of political correctness. Adults don't admit they care about being cool, but the threat of social ostracism triggers our adolescent chemistry. Cortisol makes it seem like an urgent threat, even if you're excluded from something you didn't want in the first place. Our verbal brain doesn't recognize the strength of the social dominance and herd-seeking circuits built in adolescence.

We can't just delete these core circuits, but we can rewire them with lots of repetition. I told myself that it's cool to be independent. The herd followers wish they were independent but they don't have the courage. Yes, this is adolescent sour grapes. And it doesn't even fool the mammal brain at first. Your inner mammal still seeks "popularity" as if your survival depends on it. But those old circuits are built from random experiences rather than superior wisdom. If I feed my brain new experiences repeatedly, new pathways will build. I can retrain my inner mammal to define social power in new ways.

We are often told that "our society" has destroyed social trust. The opposite is true. It is easier to trust strangers these days. We trust them with our thoughts, our money, and even our bodies. We invest less in old trust bonds because new bonds are easier to come by.

But the hell-in-a-handbasket view of social support is repeated so often that your brain may default to it. You see lapses of social trust on the news so you under-weigh the social trust that you actually have. You get idealized images about social trust in the past, so which makes your reality look bad by comparison. The truth is that our ancestors rarely left their villages because it was so unsafe. They stuck with their old ties out of fear. Today, people roam the world mingling with strangers in safety. We have more social trust than our ancestors ever dreamed of. I decided to roam the world and enjoy it instead of taking it for granted.

But I don't want to "pass" as a progressive to feel safe. I don't want a country where people with different political views have to ghettoize themselves in separate schools, separate search engines, separate comedy clubs, and separate dating sites. So I keep reminding myself that the world is full of social support that is not controlled by the gatekeepers of political correctness. That support will not just fall into my lap, though. I have to plant and nurture the seeds. When I do, I am rewarded by social connections that do not rest on fixed ideologies.

I don't want a country where people with different political views have to ghettoize themselves in separate schools, separate search engines, separate comedy clubs, and separate dating sites.

17.
How to feel safe without political correctness

It's hard to feel safe because our brain is designed to scan for threats. Political correctness helps people feel safe by promising unity in the face of threat. It offers a simple explanation for threats (social injustice) and a simple solution (fighting social injustice). When I distanced myself from political correctness, I didn't know where I would find a sense of safety.

But like kicking an addiction, I felt safer when I learned to live without it. Political correctness is like a drug, bringing you short run relief but leaving you more threatened in the long run. As you seek more relief, you end up more threatened. This is why political correctness combines easily with other addictions. People think: "Why not have another, given the state of the world today?" I rejected this short-run relief and focused on long-run safety instead.

Political correctness combines easily with other addictions. "Why not have another, given the state of the world today?"

Escaping political correctness freed me from the threatened feelings it creates. I released the belief that bad guys are oppressing me. I released the fear of being excommunicated by the politically correct. I stopped squelching of my own thoughts. I lost the safety that comes from running with the herd, but I gained the safety that comes from my own best judgment.

I lost the safety that comes from running with the herd, but I gained the safety that comes from my own best judgment.

For example, it's natural to feel threatened by illness and aging. Political correctness channels that fear into anger at the system as it impacts your health. You end up focused on the negative, which is bad for your health. I started focusing on health improvements instead of on the hell-in-a-handbasket view. To do that I have to sift information for myself because most of what's available is negative.

Violence is another significant source of threatened feelings. Political correctness requires you to blame violence on theoretical oppression rather than on actual perpetrators. It tells you that people are not responsible for their violent acts. This may feel good for a moment as you blame a common enemy, but it leaves you with a gnawing fear of unchecked violence. I decided to think for myself about violence instead of being gnawed at by the politically correct view.

Here are three simple steps that helped me feel safe without political correctness.

1. I focus on my next step

Cortisol is relieved by taking action. When a gazelle smells a predator, it acts and the threatened feeling stops. We humans find it harder to relieve threatened feelings because we think beyond immediate threats. Yet we still relieve cortisol by taking action.

Choosing your next step can feel threatening, of course, because you might take the wrong step. Fear of missteps leads people to freeze and miss out on the nice sense of relief. You have to believe in your own power in order to take a step. Political correctness trains you to believe in the power of the herd. It focuses you on colossal threats, so you feel powerless on your own. It takes the pleasure out of planning your next by suggesting that it's selfish. So you follow the steps exhorted by the leaders of political correctness, even at the expense of your own needs. You can end up feeling less safe instead of more safe.

I learned to focus on my next step by having a short-term goal, a long-term goal, and a middle-term goal. When one path seems blocked, I focus on another, so there is always a step I can take. I never let myself think that political correctness is blocking my path. If I choose a wrong at times, I just focus on my next step. Choosing it myself feels safer than letting political correctness choose it for me.

The pleasure of planning your next step is easy to understand from a baboon's perspective. If a baboon smells a predator, its survives by figuring out where the threat is coming from. It would not survive if it just ran anywhere. Once it chooses a course of action, it focuses on the ground beneath its feet. In short, it focuses on the solution rather than staring at the threat. Natural selection built a brain that rewards you with a good feeling when you focus on your next step.

Departing from political correctness can be scary at first because you've lost your simple solution. You're like a baboon who smells a predator but can't figure out where it is. Without oppression to define your sense of threat, it's hard to pick the path to safety.

Escaping political correctness makes you master of your own ship. If the ship sinks, it's your fault. This can feel threatening, so many people would rather be on someone else's ship.

Of course, it's natural to seek a powerful social alliance. It's natural to feel small without ties to a greater force. This feeling built early because we are born helpless and cannot meet our own needs. It's augmented in adolescence when your ability to meet your own needs is tested. Political correctness appeals to these deep impulses. It defines your next step in a way that's easy to follow. Soon you realize that things are more complicated, but by then you've wired yourself to feel safe by following the PC herd.

> Escaping political correctness makes you master of your own ship. Now it's your fault if the ship sinks. This can feel threatening, so many people would rather be on someone else's ship.

Political correctness defines the threat as anyone in a position of authority. It encourages you to feel that your path is blocked. A young primate can be forgiven for feeling that its access to resources is blocked by its elders, since that is often the case. The challenge faced by young chimpanzees, for example, is staggering. They are born with visible markers of juvenile status (a white tuft of fur on their bottom and pale skin on their face), and as long as those markers are visible, adults cut them slack when. In a few short years, the markers disappear and a young chimp is bitten or whacked if it violates the sensibilities of its elders. No one gives it food, so it must meet its own needs without stepping on any toes. Every species alive today has survived because its juveniles can transition out of dependency despite the frustrations. You may think animals live in a paradise of solidarity, but they are warily focused on their next step.

> A species survives because its juveniles can transition out of dependency despite the frustrations.

It's hard to feel good about meeting your own needs when you are told that "they" have failed to meet your needs for you. This is the message that young people often hear. Their teachers condemn authority because it builds bonds. Mass media purport to fight authority for you because it gets your attention. Politicians condemn rival authorities for failing to meet your needs. Such messages appeal to a young brain, and repetition wires them in. Then your brain reflexively blames "our society" for failing to meet your needs instead of focusing on your next step. It triggers outrage instead of building your power to take those steps. This is the child's view of life. It seems normal in adulthood, however, if it's accepted by those around you.

When I was young, I got A's by writing essays about what's wrong with the world. I got rewarded for criticizing, so I learned to criticize more than to solve. But as I got older, I saw that the cosmic oppression message was repeated early and often, and it was the Marxist message I'd studied in college in updated language. I did not want to be a bit player in a drama written a century ago. So instead of focusing on oppression, I focus on my next step.

2. I don't compare myself to others

Social comparison triggers threatened feelings more than we realize. The mammal brain has always compared itself to others, and the modern world feeds this impulse by filling your screens with people who seem to have ideal lives. You may oppose social comparison with your conscious mind, but it can trigger your cortisol anyway. Your mammal brain zooms in your weaknesses because that promotes survival in the state of nature.

Opinion leaders tell us that some people have everything handed to them and we are unfairly deprived. That sense of deprivation is inflamed by teaching children to expect greatness. When applause doesn't come, people end up feeling bad, even in a good life. The only solution is to recognize that social comparison comes from inside you. You can stop it there.

For example, when I read the Acknowledgment pages of other people's books, I get the feeling that these authors have armies of influential and insightful friends that I do not have. If I dwell on this, I will flood my body with cortisol. So I avoid reading those Acknowledgments. The lucky authors with all those powerful friends may have their own problems, but my focus should not be there. I focus on steps I can take to meet my needs.

I do not check my numbers. In today's world, checking your numbers is considered sound management practice, even for artists. But a neurochemical roller coaster is the likely result. Dopamine soars when a number goes up, but then that number becomes your new floor and anything less is a disappointment. I don't need that cortisol so I just focus on the pleasure of creating.

My students helped me understand the dangers of social comparison. They would often complain that "my roommate did great on a test without studying." They took this as evidence that tests are unjust and therefore they shouldn't study. Presuming injustice instead of investing effort in your skills does not keep you safe in the long run. But it feels good in the short run, which makes it popular.

The gatekeepers of political correctness promote social comparison to fuel anger. Your anger helps them, but it doesn't help you. I decided to manage my social-comparison impulse instead. I stopped believing that others have constant joy while I am somehow shortchanged.

I stopped believing that others have constant joy while I am somehow shortchanged.

The social-comparison impulse is hard to notice because it's so deeply wired. Every child has had one-up and one-down experiences. Every child notices how many cookies the other kids get. Children also mirror the social comparisons made by their elders. You may get wired to agonize over other people's cookies even when you're not hungry. You have the power to end this agony today instead of waiting for the world to change.

You may say you are just want fairness, but your brain defines fairness from the perspective of its own needs. You define justice in a way that benefits you, as much as you hate to admit it. It's even harder to admit this in public because shared grievances are the core of social bonds. But when you know the truth about mammalian social comparison, you free yourself from the belief that you are oppressed.

You define justice in a way that benefits you, as much as you hate to admit it.

Shared grievances build social bonds, but you can free yourself from the belief that you are oppressed.

---

3. I put things in historical context

We are told that today's threats are worse than ever. This is repeated so incessantly that hardly anyone questions it. But reading history makes it clear that life was much harder in the past. If I had lived in an earlier time period, I would have been assaulted by violence, physical discomfort, and social norms far more than I am today. So I choose to feel good about my life instead of spending it in a constant state of alarm.

This leaves me out of synch with prevailing beliefs. When people try to alarm me with their crisis messages, they don't seem especially interested in my historical context. They may even think I am insulting their intelligence when I fail to support their alarmism. But I still can't bring myself to put on the crisis goggles and follow the crowd. I know it is a waste of my life energy.

It's easy to see why crisis thinking is popular: it helps mass media, politicians and educators compete for our attention. People like messages that help them manage threatened feelings. We're like monkeys drinking from crocodile-infested waters. We feel better when we see the crocodile because then we can monitor it while we drink. A define threat feels better than an undefined threat. When you are told that racists and sexists are the threat to focus on, it feels safe to go back in the water.

Worrying about the state of the world distracts you from personal issues that cut deeper. You get relief when you turn on the news because it explains your anxiety in a way that's not your fault.

Worrying about the state of the world distracts you from personal issues that cut deeper. You get relief when you turn on the news because it explains your anxiety in a way that's not your fault.

You may feel obliged to share in the crisis feelings of others to avoid looking like a bad person. You turn it on when you wake up each morning by checking the news, and you keep it going all day with more news-checking. But you have a choice. You can read history from non-PC sources, and you will see how bad things were in the past. Then you can look at today with a sense of perspective. You can recognize your anxiety as the natural frustration of a mammal desperately seeking survival in a world of other mammals desperately seeking survival.

You may say we must make a better future regardless of the flaws of the past. Improving the world is a worthy goal indeed, but improvement schemes are often designed for the benefit of those advocating the program and do not really benefit others. Everyone thinks their program deserves your money because it will fix the world. They want you to believe that your survival is threatened without it. And from their perspective, their pet project does save the world because it meets their survival needs. But you don't have to believe people who confuse the greater good with their own needs.

Real solutions are hard to find despite the prognostications of experts. Throughout human history, solutions came from people who did not get immediate rewards. When you hear about great problem-solvers in history, you may think they were celebrated in their lifetime, but they were often ridiculed and attacked. Problems got solved because they persisted without applause.

Problems got solved because people persisted without applause or rewards.

So instead of getting snared by the climate of alarm, you can plant seeds for solutions you believe in. Keep watering those seeds instead of expecting the gatekeepers of political correctness to water them for you. You may think your seeds are wrongfully neglected while politically correct seeds get fertilized. If you think this way, you will not take the steps that your seeds need to flourish. Just keep taking steps.

I used to be addicted to negativity about the state of the world. I stopped because I lived in the sausage factory and saw how the sausage was made. I even participated in making it by alarming my students about various "crises." But the more I saw that crisis messages get rewards, the less I believed those messages.

I understand the allure of the crisis mentality because I was lured by it myself. It's easy to believe that the world is in crisis when your cortisol is flowing. You can't imagine that your brain turned it on for self-interested reasons like a disappointed quest for social importance. It helps to remember that the mammal brain sees obstacles to your social importance as survival threats. If you had what you think others have, your happy chemicals would still sag after they spurt. Your cortisol would still be triggered by disappointment. Everyone has these frustrations, even people who are designated as "privileged." Instead of mourning lost illusions of grandeur, you can enjoy your power to choose your next step.

Political correctness triggers your cortisol in many ways. It commands you to ignore tangible threats and banishes you if you acknowledge them. It destroys your trust in institutions that are effectively protecting you. It insists that your threatened feelings are evidence of oppression. You end up feeling more threatened when you turn to political correctness for safety. This addiction cannot be fixed by more political correctness. Escaping it is a big relief.

18.
How to lead without political correctness

Leadership feels good because it puts you in the one-up position. We're not supposed to care about that, but it stimulates your serotonin, which wires you to seek more of it. With so few socially acceptable ways to feel one-up, so leadership is highly desired.

Political correctness disdains authority but it celebrates leaders who give "power to the people." Such leaders claim to meet people's needs, as defined by the people themselves. This kind of leadership feels good to everyone in the short run, but it has some harmful consequences in the long run.

Politically correct leadership becomes a popularity contest. You may find yourself leading in a direction you know is wrong because you're afraid of losing popularity. Leaders have always confronted this dilemma, of course. They have always protected their own interests by deferring to the squeakiest wheel, justifying it by invoking the greater good. Today's leaders say they're empowering the people when they yield to the squeakiest wheel. They're called Nazis if they don't yield, and lose their one-up position.

I call this "nice-ism": the belief that being nice to everyone will make them nice to you. Nice-ism gets a bad result sometimes, and leaders are supposed to respond by being even nicer. Thus not-nice behaviors get rewarded. People quickly observe what behaviors get rewarded, so nice-ist leadership can increase bad behavior. You may be enabling your most authoritarian subordinates in your quest to avoid looking authoritarian.

When things go wrong, the "nice" leader blames higher-ups. This provides a common enemy for the group to bond around. It's a way to win the support of your group despite dysfunctional outcomes. You set the tone of blaming those upstairs instead of taking responsibility. This kind of leadership cedes power to those who complain the loudest.

The urge to maintain your leadership position is natural because it gives you a sense of control in an uncertain world. Leading a battle against common enemies is more fun than taking responsibility for your mammalian hostility toward those "enemies." It's hard to resist the temptation of politically correct leadership.

But one day your cheerleader approach will cause enough pain to make you question it. This happened to me in my leadership of students and family. I realized that I was not helping them; I was only helping my fear of being called a Nazi. If I cared about others, I would assert my best judgment even if it was not popular. Here's how I did it.

1. Enforce rules equally

Everyone talks about equality, but the word is often used to advocate for special privileges. That's the opposite of equality, but no one dares to say so.

Modern leaders give lip service to the principle that the rules apply to everyone, but they tend to bend the rules to accommodate special pleading. When you are a leader, you are flooded with requests for exceptions to the rules. If you stick to the rules, people say you're not nice— in nastier language.

> Everyone talks about equality, but the word is often used to advocate for special privileges. That's the opposite of equality, but no one dares to say so.

Most people like the rule of law until it's applied to them. Then they feel like some injustice has been done. For example, you see that parking rules are necessary to make parking spaces available, but when you get a parking ticket, you feel wronged. No one openly says they think they're above the law, but many people learn from early experience to expect exemptions.

Political correctness suggests that you are entitled to violate the rules because the system is unjust. Undermining the system of rules is even viewed as an accomplishment. This view has obvious appeal to young people and those who seek popularity with young people. But it destroys the social capital that our ancestors took centuries to build. Impunity hurts everyone.

Political correctness suggests that you are entitled to violate the rules because the system is unjust. This destroys the social capital that our ancestors took centuries to build.

I took the rule of law for granted until I lived in countries that lacked it. I saw the electricity and water systems fail because the money allotted to them was stolen. Poverty was blamed for collapsing infrastructure, but foreign-aid money had been given to these leaders over and over, and they stole it each time. Aid agencies were too "progressive" to enforce the rules, so people lived without water and electricity. I finally realized how much has gone right when our infrastructure works. My "good education" trained me to critique these systems, but I finally learned that courageous enforcement of rules is necessary to keep a system functioning.

Many of my students came from countries where you have to bribe to get a driver's license. A bribe gets you a license delivered to your home even if you never took a single driving lesson. Many students seemed pleased with this "customer service," and with their own bribery skills. They ignored the long-run price of corruption because the short-run reward is so tangible.

Courageous enforcement of rules is necessary to keep a system functioning.

Economists call our attention to "the tragedy of the commons," and the "agency problem." But in my good education, these theories were always illustrated with politically correct examples such as corporate greed. The potential for corruption among the politically correct cannot be mentioned without risking excommunication. This reinforces the belief that all problems are caused by the right and are solved by fighting the right. When the rules are broken by the politically correct, it is always justified as evening the score. And when "right wingers" are accused of breaking the rules, no evidence seems necessary because you already "know" they are corrupt. I am surrounded by this view of law enforcement, so it took me decades to transcend it.

You can see corruption among the politically correct if you dare to look. Progressives yield to the agency problem and the tragedy of the commons just like other mammals. When college professors give out grades that students haven't earned, they meet their own needs, but harm those who pay the bills. Leadership means risking unpopularity to enforce rules equally.

People learn their expectations about rule enforcement from their leaders. I learned this in an unusual way. When I caught my students cheating, I reported it according to university policy. My colleagues rarely did this, and advised me to do likewise. Then new rules were introduced that saying a student could only be charged with cheating if course syllabus defines cheating. This was based on the assertion that many of our students grew up in countries where school work is done cooperatively (the superior way, according to my colleagues), so they do not think they are cheating. Most professors chose not to define cheating in their syllabus. They feared looking like a Nazi in print. They just continued to ignore cheating. But I put cheating guidelines in my syllabus and worked to build a system with integrity in my classroom.

The rule of law works with carrots and sticks. You get carrots for abiding by the rules, and sticks for violating them. Sticks are hard to enforce in the politically correct world, so the rule of law depends on the drive to earn carrots. But that drive is weak when you are taught that carrots should be free, and that violating the rules is glorious. The rule of law is a precious tradition that is being eviscerated by politically correct messages. Leaders can boost their popularity by giving out free carrots while disavowing the stick (except for "right-wingers"). The "free" carrots are paid for by the productivity of people who live by the rules.

Carrots become less motivating when you get them easily. This is a serious dilemma for leaders who are too nice to use sticks. When your group learns to think the rules don't apply to them, it gets stuck in a place defined by the least cooperative person in the group. The only solution is to retrain people to expect the rules to apply to everyone. You will have to explain the rules over and over to protect yourself from accusations.

2. Acknowledge uncertainty

In a data-driven world, we presume that all problems are predictable. Leaders are blamed for problems because they're expected to prevent them. Leaders strive to protect themselves from blame by anticipating and averting problems. But things go wrong that are not predicted by their forecasting tools. No one likes to acknowledge uncertainty, but we end up in a blame game if we don't.

Pretending that life is statistically predictable motivates us to focus on predictable problems. This is the dilemma of Total Quality Management. It succeeded at improving quality and reducing costs, but it led to defensiveness that is counter-productive. People are so eager to look good in ways that are measured that they ignore facts that don't fit popular measures. Embracing uncertainty does not mean shirking blame; it means staying open to information that is not officially tracked.

A simple example is the problem of addiction. Many conflicting theories of its causes and cures are warring against each other. Each camp points to "the data" to support its case, and sneers at others for ignoring "the data." The low success rates of addiction treatments are ignored because they reflect badly on those leading the discussion. Instead of acknowledging uncertainties about addiction, they blame "our society." Attacking a common enemy, like "stigmatizing" and lack of "compassion," helps leaders build confidence when solutions are unknown.

No one likes to acknowledge uncertainty because it seems weak. Leaders are tempted blame accepted bad guys instead of confronting unknowns. Energy is spent defending old positions unless until a leader courageously explores the unknown.

3. Focus on the positive

The beer-and-pizza school of motivation allows the most negative people to set the pace for everyone. It expects leaders to "empathize" with grievances regardless of their validity. A leader risks being accused of an "ism" if they don't. Negatives suck up energy that could have been invested in positives.

It's easier to focus on the positive when you distance yourself from the herd. I was thrilled to be a waitress at a steakhouse when I was in college because I earned triple the pay of a campus job, and got exercise while going it. Yet everyone I know saw the job as a negative. Today, food servers are routinely depicted as victims of oppression, and students are not expected to work at such jobs. We trained people to look for subtle slights, and to rage at them. This prepares them to serve in the army of discontent rather than to meet their future needs. If I had haughty customers when I was a waitress, I didn't even notice because I was too busy meeting my needs.

It's easier to critique what others are building than to build something yourself. If you invest your energy in criticizing, it may feel good in the short-run but you build nothing for the long run.

We all get to choose where we focus. Those choices are heavily influenced by where our leaders focus. I was not a real leader in my early years. I focused on criticizing in a way that taught my students and my children to criticize. I wish I had noticed this habit sooner. But eventually, I learned to make a new choice. We are all lucky to have a choice.

Epilogue

The day I lost my cool

I've filled this book with reasonable responses so it's only fair to add the story of the day I lost it. It was the year 2000, and I had a brand-new husband. He was telling me that his son's Spanish teacher was no good, and I asked him how he knew that. He said his son told him so.

What?!?! Your only evidence is the gripe of an interested party— a child who is failing the course? I exploded with rage when I heard that.

This seems like a big reaction for a small comment. After all I'd been through, why did that statement push me over the edge?

I hate to see young people trained to blame the teacher when things don't go their way. Admittedly there's self-interest since I'm a teacher. But it seems like a short step from there to blaming your ill health on the health care system, your lack of money on the bank, your lack of inner peace on the government, and all your other disappointments on racist-sexist-elitist-homophobic-Islamophobic-Nazi-hater-bigots.

No one benefits in the long run from making others responsible for their lives. A striking example came to my attention when I was a Zoo Docent. People often asked about animals escaping the zoo, but the interesting fact is that animals break in more than they break out.

They don't break out because animals defend their turf. They feel threatened by new turf. They only break out when a zoo acquires a new animal and a dominance struggle turns life-threatening.

Animals break in all the time because food is just lying around in a zoo. Imagine you were a wild gazelle looking through the fence at a zoo gazelle enjoying a big pile of food. Your dopamine soars and you jump over the fence into the zoo. At first you are thrilled with the relief from hunger and the protection from predators. But after a while your happy chemicals sag. They evolved to reward steps that meet needs, so they're not stimulated if no steps are necessary.

Your lost happiness seems like the zookeepers' fault because you've learned to expect them to meet your needs. You get angry at them, but nothing changes. Finally you are so frustrated that you want to break out. But maybe you've lost confidence in your ability to navigate the world of predator threat and competitive herd mates.

Of course, real gazelles do not expect a promised land where good feelings flow effortlessly. But modern humans have learned to expect constant happiness, and condemn the system when disappointed. This habit of blaming externals undermines your internal power. You can make peace with your inner mammal instead. There will be good teachers and bad teachers in your life; good bosses and bad bosses; good service and bad service. If you blame your outcomes on others, you will not build the skills you need to have better outcomes. You become a sacrifice to the gods of political correctness. I could not stand by and let that happen to a child in my home, and I let my new husband know it.

It saddens me when people stop believing in their own agency. I hoped that brain research would help people recognize their own power, but the opposite often happens. Brain research is used to reinforce the "it's not your fault" message. It feeds the expectation of an external fix instead of building internal self-management skills.

After I lost my cool, I worked harder to co-exist with political correctness. I'm happy to say that I stayed calm in a more difficult moment. My father was dying and I was sitting with him in the hospital looking for something useful to do. It was fall, so I offered to get him an absentee ballot. Later, I told my brother and he said "Don't do that. He'll vote for Bush." In the past I would have just feigned agreement with my brother, but I screwed up my courage and gently said, "it's his right."

You may wish I'd said more. You may wish I'd said less. But it worked out. We had a talk that finally revealed why my parents never mentioned politics: my mother was a Democrat and my father was a Republican. They knew their votes cancelled each other out, and even considered staying home on Election Day. But neither trusted the other to honor the bargain.

I was thrilled to share that moment of authenticity with my brother. We both live in a world where progressives view others as "the enemy." I feared that my brother would treat me as the enemy, but I didn't yield to that fear. I took a risk, I kept the door open, and we both walked through it.

I don't want a one-party system. After the long human struggle for democracy, I will not support a culture that ostracizes people who don't vote "the right way."

Escaping political correctness does not mean insisting you're right and telling others they're wrong. It means focusing on the path in front of you instead of on the herd.

We learn to expect constant happiness, and condemn the system when disappointed. This habit of blaming externals undermines your internal power.

Keep in Touch

Has this book helped you? Please tell me what you did that worked: Loretta@InnerMammalInstitute.org

For more information on building your power over your mammalian brain chemistry, check out the many free resources of the Inner Mammal Institute, and our very approachable books. InnerMammalInstitute.org

Videos
"You Have Power Over Your Brain," at:
YouHavePowerOverYourBrain.com.

Social media
Facebook: facebook.com/LorettaBreuningPhD/
Twitter: @innermammal
Discussion group:
facebook.com/groups/InnerMammalInstitute/

Books
- Habits of a Happy Brain: Retrain your brain to boost your serotonin, dopamine, oxytocin and endorphin
- The Science of Positivity: Stop Negative Thought Patterns By Changing Your Brain Chemistry
- I, Mammal: How to Make Peace With the Animal Urge for Social Power
- Anxiety: What Turns It On. What Turns It Off.

About the Author

Loretta Graziano Breuning, PhD is Professor Emerita of Management at California State University, East Bay, and founder of the Inner Mammal Institute.

Her work has been featured on Forbes, NPR, Time, Psychology Today, Wall St Journal, Cosmopolitan, Fast Company, Men's Health, NBC, Real Simple, Dr Oz, and a wide range of podcasts. It has been translated into Spanish, Russian, Chinese, French, Arabic and Turkish. The Inner Mammal Institute offers free resources that help you build power over your mammalian brain chemistry.

Dr. Breuning's many books, videos, blogs, and digital resources have helped thousands of people make peace with their inner mammal. Her previous books include:

- Habits of a Happy Brain: Retrain your brain to boost your serotonin, dopamine, oxytocin and endorphin

- The Science of Positivity: Stop Negative Thought Patterns By Changing Your Brain Chemistry

- I, Mammal: How to Make Peace With the Animal Urge for Social Power

- Anxiety: What Turns It On. What Turns It Off

CPSIA information can be obtained
at www.ICGtesting.com
Printed in the USA
LVOW13s1741220218
567560LV00013B/1420/P

9 781941 959114